Mastering the Law of Attraction

by

Andy Shaw

November 2014

Andy Shaw

Published and distributed in the United Kingdom by www.AndyShaw.com

This book is designed to provide competent and reliable information regarding the subject matter covered. However, it is sold with the understanding that the author and publisher are not engaged in rendering legal, financial, or other professional advice. Laws vary from country to country and if legal or other expert assistance is required, the services of a professional should be sought. The author and publisher specifically disclaim any liability that is incurred from the use or application of the contents of this book.

Contents

Introduction:

What You Can Expect To Get

The law of attraction is not about knowing that it exists and learning more and more stuff about it. It's about getting you real life results, and that's what I intend for this book to do for you today.

My intention with Mastering the Law of Attraction is to a) demonstrate why the law of attraction always works and, if you've found it doesn't, then b) explain EXACTLY how to use it so it always does for you from now on. Also c) to teach you how to become a master practitioner of it, so you can get all you desire from life.

Does that sound good?

Well, before going any further, just for a few seconds I'd like you to imagine it happening…

I want you to pause now and just for 30 seconds choose to see yourself as **someone who can make it work** and who, is in fact a master practitioner of the law of attraction…

But before you pause, you'll probably have a voice in your head saying *'not to kid yourself,'* or perhaps you'll just doubt that you're capable of achieving it. That's okay! We'll fix that faulty thinking later… For now, what I'd like you to do is, just for the next 30 seconds, imagine that you <u>ARE</u> that person. Just tell the voice in your head to give you a break and allow you to dream for a few seconds and maybe do a deal with the voice and say you'll let it go back to doubting all this later on.

Yes, I know, talking to yourself is supposed to be a bit insane. But I suggest if you wish to become a master practitioner of the law of attraction, then you may just want to go with this. I suggest you relax and allow me the time to explain everything to you as we go through… Is that okay?

So now, just for a few seconds, *dare to dream.* See yourself in say a few years time as someone who is a master of the law of attraction. Don't look at the stuff you created over the next few years, instead just see yourself as someone who has done it and enjoy that feeling for at least 15 seconds, without any doubt being present. Pause now and do it.

Here's what to expect...

I created this course to make you a master of this wonderful law of attraction tool we have all been given. So the idea is by the end of it you'll have the skill set required to become and be the master you were actually designed to be. Yes, you were designed to be naturally successful, so it's not that hard for me to get you back on track, despite what you may currently think.

During this short course, I'm going to share with you some stories of the numerous things I've manifested using the law of attraction and I'm going to share a few stories of what my students have achieved doing it too. I promise you that their stories are from down to Earth people who are just using the structured thinking techniques I teach to achieve some pretty impressive stuff.

I'm going to give you all the structured thinking techniques which will allow you to use the law of attraction to get you what you want, instead of accidental thinking which mostly gets you more of what you don't want. So look out for those techniques as we go through, because the results you'll get when applying them really will blow you away. And they are quick and easy to learn.

Before I give you some of the key techniques though, I want to give you plenty of proof that this technique I use, is working for me and my students. When I show you the techniques, I want you to accept it as *real* and most importantly know that *you have this power too.*

I'm also going to get you to consider some things as we go along... as when I get you to think for a while you change your thinking pattern, which, to go technical for a few moments is about brain plasticity. As you change your thinking, it becomes easier to accept things which you have previously doubted. Then I will prove to you, those doubts are literally killing your dreams.

My intention is to get your brain changing whilst we are going through these techniques, so that your default way of thinking is to use the law of attraction to progress your life. You don't need to really know much about brain plasticity (thank goodness), just that it works and will work to your benefit if you follow the techniques I'm going to teach you.

Just so you know, until recently the brain was seen as a rather static organ, but it's now clear that the organisation of brain circuitry is **constantly changing as a function of experience**. So the easiest way to alter your thinking is simply by putting up a signpost in your mind and getting you to consider something when you see the sign... That's about as complicated as I'm going to make this, okay?

I'm also going to show you something that should blow you away and shake the foundations of all you currently think you know... When I do that, you'll see that "knowing" the law of attraction exists and "knowing" how you're supposed to use it does not equate to you being able to use it. In fact, it can prevent your ability to use it.

When I'm finished explaining this all to you, it will make it impossible for you to not become a master of the law of attraction. This is because *I like to make it harder for you to fail, than it is for you to succeed.* That way, as humans we always default to the easy way, and the easy way for you is going to *always equal success...* So now does that sound very good?

A little about me & why I can teach this to you...

My Great Uncle Dave gave me the greatest gift anyone could ever give me in 1980, when I was 13 years old. He told me I was going to be a millionaire and I was going to have a great life. I had a few bits missing from what I needed to succeed, but not to worry, as the people I needed would come to me. They would come into my life as I needed them, and that all I needed to do was notice them and look for a way to get them to help me.

I asked him how would I know them, and he said to me that they would have a sign on their head. What he meant by that was that I would feel they were being sent to help me and I can honestly say that they do, I see the sign the first time I meet them. I just don't always recognise it because sometimes, in my past, I've been too busy.

I started in business in my early 20's and people viewed us as a big success by my early 30's, although I wasn't what I considered rich and, one day, I noticed that I wasn't yet the millionaire my Uncle Dave had predicted. So I set about becoming rich and set myself the ridiculous goal of being a millionaire in two years. I became a millionaire about six months later and a multi-millionaire just two weeks later. Within the first year I'd made over £5,000,000, probably nearer £10,000,000.

Later, I wondered why I'd achieved such a "bad goal" so spectacularly and I realised that I wasn't chasing the money, my true reason why, was I wanted the kudos of being able to call myself a millionaire, and to prove my uncle was right.

Nearly two years after my first big success, I read my 'first' personal development book called Rich Dad Poor Dad. At the time, people were coming up to me and virtually begging me to teach them how I became rich so fast. I said that I didn't need to teach them, that the formula was written down in that book and they could learn it from that. The next book I read was Think and Grow Rich, and the formula was in there too, as it was in all success books.

After a few months people started coming back to me disillusioned and saying that those books didn't work for them. This shocked me, as I had to get rich on my own, I didn't know you could just read a book and do it. That way was much easier... So I was baffled, I knew those books worked and had the formula, but why couldn't they get it to work? This really made me curious...

Then, in 2004, I attended my first seminar. I didn't know you could carry on learning after school... Yes, I wasn't very smart! So, if you're at least smarter than that, then you're laughing! I was at this seminar with exactly 100 people in it when I first heard the fact that *only 1% of people ever succeed at getting what they want in life...* Now this really blew me away!

Instantly I thought, *'what are the rest of you all doing here as I'm the 1% in this room.'* I then began to wonder why people would attempt success in life, when the odds were so stacked against them. As I'd never play a game with those odds, that would be mad... But they all seemed to be doing it.

This all made me furious, as I knew I could succeed and would succeed... They were all learning exactly the same things as me but I knew that they wouldn't be able to succeed where I could... So then the question came out of me that changed the course of my life and ended up costing me my entire first fortune in 2009.

I asked myself, *"Why can I succeed, and why can't they?"* I meant why couldn't 99% of people succeed. It doesn't look much like an expensive question does it? Well that question cost me well over $30 million!

Eventually, I got my answer and that led to me creating my A Bug Free Mind Process in 2010. I found out why people couldn't succeed and it turned out to be something really simple... I learnt that the world had been taught *what to think*, and not *how to think*.

How to think is left to chance and is therefore *without structure*, whereas what to think information is piled into a head which has no system for thinking. So, paralysed by stacks of information, and with no system to regulate and use the information to get what they want, means that people worry, become afraid, get depressed, get stressed, get overwhelmed, and can't apply what they learnt to get what they want... and, amongst many other things, usually only use the law of attraction to create bad stuff.

They could learn and feel good from learning what people taught them but just couldn't quite get it to work... So I realised there was a problem with the way success was being taught. My epiphany moment was when I figured out that I had, inside my head, the missing piece of the puzzle.

So I created the Bug Free Mind Process. My ulterior motive for giving you this course on Mastering the Law of Attraction is that you will take it, see that it can work for you and you'll be curious enough to see how much more I can teach you in the full Bug Free Mind Process… I also intend to give you probably the most valuable and applicable information you've found so far… Is that okay?

My curiosity eventually gave me the answer but cost me tens of millions to get it. That curiosity has led to you being here reading this today. Maybe after you see some results, then you'll see that I can help you create a life full of success in all areas of life.

The other irritation I became curious about was when I found that only 1% of people succeed with personal development books too. This wound me up, as I thought I must do better and teach things in a way my dad taught me.

He was a teacher and one day I was struggling to learn something my maths teacher had shown me. He showed me the way again and I still didn't understand it. So he showed me it another way and I got it. I asked him why my maths teacher hadn't shown me the way he had and he said to me that, *"it is the teacher's job to teach it in a way that the student can understand and learn it. It is not the student's job to figure out what the teacher means."*

So thanks to this powerful gift my dad gave me, I will teach that way to you. In the process of teaching that way, *I repeat things on purpose* and this is why I have an extremely high success rate in my teachings (over 92% in fact, not good enough but I think you'll agree somewhat better than the standard 1%).

And to enhance your reading, this was written in October 2014. I am British and live in West Sussex UK. I'm married to my perfect partner Alison who, much to her disgust, I used the law of attraction to find when I was 21 years old.

I have two children, David 15 and Sarah 12. In my career I have gone from a C grade student to cabinet maker, to business owner, to multi, multi-millionaire investor. To broke, to multi-millionaire again. I've had massive successes and massive failures and been involved in dozens of businesses… *I have a lot of 'T' shirts!'*

Lastly, before we begin… If you are looking for a well-crafted piece of English literature that will be a pleasure to read and leave you feeling good but not leave you as a master of the law of attraction… then this isn't it. I'm blunt and to the point, I teach in a way designed to get you thinking by altering the pattern you use to think right now, so that you change your results in the shortest possible time.

I am going to keep this as short as possible but I will not shorten this if I think it will affect the teaching and therefore your implementation of it. If I think I need to tell you something ten times to get a point over, I will do. It's my job as the teacher to get you results.

If that's okay with you, then let's begin.

Oh, I'll also make you feel good too and teach you a fair few things, which you secretly already knew, but you couldn't be certain of... So you are going to enjoy this a lot and get results as well. Shall we begin?

The first lesson then is this...

As you go through this short process, you are to *choose to always be delighted with yourself*. When you feel yourself getting annoyed with yourself for not achieving something, not applying something, not knowing something, then you are to catch yourself in the moment and choose to stop and think for just a few seconds...

If you feel like it, then say this to yourself, *"I'm not delighted with myself right now and that isn't helping me, the past is the past. I'm delighted with myself for noticing that I was not delighted with myself."*

This is a very simple thought structure; you are turning discomfort into comfort and the law of attraction is wholly reliant on your mind being one of calmness and self control. So you are going to practise calming and controlling your mind. After all, *there is no benefit in you being annoyed with yourself,* so you can choose (if you want to) to always be delighted with yourself instead...

Consider it now for a few seconds, see yourself not being delighted with something you haven't done and then choose to change your thinking to being delighted with yourself instead. How you choose to think is under your control, despite what the voice in your mind will attempt to make you think... More on that, later.

Pause now and choose to be delighted with yourself... Then move on to chapter one, the law of attraction...

Chapter 1:

The Law of Attraction

To keep this short, quantum physics has already proved that you can affect things with just thought. That's in a lab, not hocus pocus, not me just saying it... Real stuff!

If you want to go onto YouTube and search *'the double slit experiment.'* Then you'll see an experiment that's been done multiple times and proves that *matter is affected just by looking at it.* Which is what we wish to achieve with the law of attraction.

So, if we can affect things just by thought, then how much more can we do with our minds? Well, as I'll show you later on, I've found this to be virtually creating the impossible. But, I'm getting ahead of myself! The law of attraction is about manifesting, and that is making things happen with your mind. This is something, which we all can do!

A few of us are good at making good stuff happen and most people are good at manifesting bad stuff... But we are all manifestors! We just have different levels of skills when using the law of attraction in our lives.

Alexander Graham Bell, most famous for his invention of the telephone, said about the law of attraction, *"What this power is, I cannot say. All I know is that it exists."*

The film, The Secret, really brought the law of attraction into the mainstream and has been seen by well over 200 million people. Plus (I'm guessing now) there are probably another few hundred million people who've studied it a little or a lot in books and courses.

So a fair percentage of the world's population knows of it and understands it. But it's not just a modern day philosophy...

5,200 years ago, Krishna said, "When a person is devoted to something with complete faith, I unify his faith in that. Then, when his faith is completely unified, he gains the object of his devotion."

2,500 plus years ago, Buddha said, *"What we are today comes from our thoughts of yesterday, and our present thoughts build our life of tomorrow: Our life is the creation of our mind."*

2,000 years ago, Jesus Christ, said, *"Whatever you ask in prayer, believe that you have received it, and it will be yours."*

1,400 years ago, the Prophet Muhammad, said, *"Actions are judged by intentions, so each man will have what he intended."*

I could go back to every spiritual teacher and they would all tell you about the law of attraction in their own words. So this is not something new, and this is not something religious, this is not something that a group of teachers have *thought up* to sell some books. It just is! And one day it will become accepted and considered 'the norm'.

However, you have the choice of deciding if that's right or not, now. It is not my right to force you to make a choice one way or the other. I will merely show you the *benefits and costs* of your choices.

So do you think it helps you in mastering the law of attraction to choose that *this is something real and you can control it if you learn how?*

Or do you think it helps you in mastering the law of attraction to choose to *not believe it is real and therefore cannot help you?*

When it comes down to the mind, the secret is to go with what benefits you…

So which one benefits you?

However, you do not need to 'believe' as that takes effort, and I'm not a fan of effort in that direction. So all you need to do is choose that it is of benefit to you and that it is real, that's all.

Consider this, you can choose to just do that for now, you can always change your mind later… Does that now feel okay to you? You get all the benefit without any of the commitment, as all that matters is the benefit… Do you agree?

You may wish to pause to consider that for a little while and then come to this conclusion for yourself, because it's much more powerful that way. But as with everything, that's your choice, I can only tell you what will help. You have to decide to apply it to receive the help. It's a choice, and choice will always be the problem and the solution!

People used to say to me all the time, *"Do you really 'believe' in the law of attraction, Andy?"* No I don't 'believe' it, I know it – I **choose** to know it exists! This is not faith, I do not need faith to know that gravity exists even though I cannot see, hear, touch, taste or smell it.

Whatever you think is right, is right. I'll explain that to a greater depth later but a quick example is… My mum recently asked me if I thought a particular supplement would help her health, and I said, *"If you think it will, then it will!"*

You do not consciously 'need' to 'believe' in it, nor do you consciously need to 'know' it. However, you do consciously 'need' to not let 'not believing' or 'not knowing' get in your way of creating your desires, although knowing it really makes stuff easy. But that's your choice.

The law of attraction is simply a tool and, like every tool I ever used as a craftsman, it came with a manual. The manual was next to useless in making you an expert in the use of the tool and merely acted as a guide, so that you didn't stick, say, the chisel in your eye.

The real manual we create ourselves as we use the tool. As time passed, I became a better master of the tools I used and, when I spent time using a particular tool, then I became an advanced master of that. It is the same here. You are going to become a master with the law of attraction, because you are going to create a manual for yourself as you become a better craftsman.

As I said, we are all using the law of attraction all of the time. If you desire to know how good a craftsman you are with it right now, then just look at your life. But WAIT, you must not be quick to judge yourself here. I said look, I did not say judge, as there will be stacks of examples in your life right now of how you have used this tool in the most masterful ways to create what you desire. I'm talking about the good stuff, not the crud!

Some of these will be stunning examples of which others are looking to achieve. Not necessarily about money. So, in order to use the tool properly, you use it in exactly the same way as you have mastered its use before, in other areas.

You simply have to look and see how you used it to achieve what you achieved. Then you simply can apply the same techniques to the other areas of your life, which you feel are lacking.

So we all have this wonderful tool at our disposal. However, just to complicate and, *later,* simplify things for you... A better way to describe the law of attraction is as the law of creation.

Sure we get into vibrational alignment with what we want, and like attracts like... But what happens is we actually create the outcome we want in our mind by setting the vibration. We are all creators of our own lives though, right now, you may not want to hear that, if your creation isn't going according to plan.

But just go with it and remain delighted with yourself, as later on I'm going to show you how you being the creator means that you can alter your results for real... So please don't shoot me yet.

The law of attraction is not about wishful thinking, it is about using structured thought to create the outcome you desire. Just as I fix depression, worry, fear, anxiety, stress, overwhelm and all pain in life with structured thought in the A Bug Free Mind Process, you will use structured thought here to become a master of the law of attraction.

As Earl Nightingale said, *"Whatever we plant in our subconscious mind and nourish with repetition and emotion, will one day become a reality."* This is an act of creation, not attraction. Well, in my opinion, anyway!

Energy is, Matter is not.

What that means is that energy is all there is. Everything is made up of pure energy and, depending on which expert you read, then either all of the matter in all of the entire star system could be squashed down to the size of a pea, or that there is no matter at all. Wow, this is mind-blowing stuff! Isn't this stuff fascinating?

Now don't judge it, just observe. Keep something inside you observing your reactions to what you are about to read. Don't judge your reactions, just observe them. *Judgement is weakness, observation is power!*

Personally, I have more trouble with the 'pea' sized amount of matter than the concept of no matter at all. Either way, and without judgement, we are just part of one great, great, great BIG sea of energy which, as proved by the double slit experiment, shows that *'little old us'*, each affects it *'on purpose or not'* merely by thinking about it!!!

Personally, I think science proving the law of attraction once and for all exists is one of the greatest discoveries ever made, as it stops the 'absolute' argument once and for all. As my friend would say, *"I want some actual physical proof."* Well you got it! The law of attraction is more real than the chair you are sitting in!

So what does this experiment really prove? It proves that we can affect things with just our thoughts. Now I'm sure that most of people studying this sort of work will have already instinctively known this. Yet, perhaps you didn't dare to 'believe' it was really possible to do on purpose as, if you did dare, then that would mean you were a 'loony'. But we actually can! We can literally create whatever we desire in our lives. In truth, we of course are already creating it… We are just creating it by accident. The truth I think you will soon come to accept it is, that you are in direct control and the purpose of this course is to put you in control *on purpose* this time!

Talking about the Double Slit experiment for a second. The physicists basically showed that one particle of matter actually went everywhere it was possible to go, all at the same time! In other words, all possibilities happened all at once. Now this is clearly way, way off the comfortable map where we understand what's going on. So, to bring it back to more comprehensible practical stuff -

What you 'want' - the life you desire - already exists, you just need to desire it and focus on it in the correct way to bring it into your reality.

To do this deliberately, you must act as if you already have what you desire, because, of course, you already do have it! If it can happen, if it can be conceived, then it has already happened and it can be a reality for you. You just need to bring it into your physical reality consciously...

Too difficult, huh? Well you've brought your current reality into reality already - that didn't just happen! You already know how to do it; you are just doing it by accident so all you need to learn is how to do it on purpose. This really is all you need to do, to create exactly what you desire. You just need to look at what you did right in certain areas of your life and copy that into the areas you desire more.

Lack, limitation, doubt and unworthiness, all set up blocks which are not in harmony with creating what you desire. Yet they are predominantly in use in the VAST majority of people... Which is, of course, why they don't get what they desire, as you have and as I have.

We literally create our own reality, that's each of us. Yes, <u>you are</u> fully responsible and that's right, luck really does not exist! We really do live in our own little worlds but grasping this concept or fully understanding this stuff is *a) not possible* and *b) not even necessary*.

You just need to *know it's real*, or even just *know that it might be real*, then you can create your chosen outcome.

Beating the odds...

But getting back to the film The Secret... What I always wondered was, it's been seen by 200 million people, why aren't there millions of millionaires out there? People have been shown it, and taught it after all... Surely, isn't that enough?

Well according to Wikipedia, in 2012, there were only 12 million millionaires in the entire world... And millionaire isn't that rich, as that's assets worth just $1 million, not including their own home.

And $1 million is a lot of money to some people, but that's not what I consider to be rich in terms of money. But then again, the richest man is not the man who has the most, but the one who needs the least...

Do you realise that the odds of a person achieving the goal of becoming a millionaire in today's world of over 7.2 billion people are about 600 to 1...

Consider this, would you bet on a horse with odds of 600 to 1? No way, right? You'd lose all the money you bet... Well consider this, *you are betting your life on it, if you want to become a millionaire* – that's 600 – 1!

But to be very rich, you become an 'Ultra-High Net Worth Individual' and this is someone with assets of over $30 million.

According to Wikipedia, in 2013, there were just 199,235 of those in the world... Meaning the odds against that are over 36,000 to 1...

Would you bet your life on a 36,000 to 1 outsider? Well, if you're trying to get rich, that's the odds...

I achieved this and beat those odds years ago, before losing it all. So consider this, is this something you want to achieve too? As that's a lot more money than you need to live a fabulous life of ease and enjoyment.

You may wish to consider, do you want to spend your life attempting to beat those odds, just to get rich. Or would you rather spend your life doing what you love and get somewhere on the rich scale instead... As to beat the odds, you're going to need to become a master of the law of attraction...

Chapter 2:

The Unlimited Power of Thought

Henry Ford *said, "Whether you think you can or think you can't, either way you're right."* The truth is that *'thoughts'* are the most powerful thing we have at our disposal, despite what it appears.

Over the course of this, I am going to prove to you beyond question that, *'if you think you can, you can and, if you doubt you can, then you can't!'*

You can intellectually 'believe' this right now, sure... but when you live it daily as *a way of life*, then you have become a master of thinking and you can then get anything you want...

It is one thing to know it, and it is another thing entirely to live it. And that is what mastering the law of attraction is going to show you how to do.

Consider this, *whatever is going on in your mind, you are creating into your reality.*

Just consider it for a few seconds... You're not looking for conclusions, you're just looking at it and, as you consider it for a few moments, you are altering the wiring in your mind.

So, what that means is; you become and create what your dominant thoughts are. Thinking about what you don't want, creates that in your life.

Let's say you're in debt. If you think about getting out of debt, you create debt. So you have to alter your thinking to use the law of attraction to be rid of debt. I'll cover how to be free of debt later, as an example. But I wanted to use debt to make the point.

Your thoughts govern your life! Do you agree? Or do you think you are not the controller and are just a puppet? Because if you think you are just a puppet, then you may as well quit this now. As the puppet relies on luck to govern their life, the master understands chance and knows how to stack the deck of chance in his or her favour.

So are you the controller or the puppet?

Don't just say the answer, feel it...
Consider, would quitting benefit you, or would mastering the law of attraction benefit you...

Therefore, your choice is surely to agree that your thoughts govern your life. So it's essential to comprehend that careful choice of thoughts is required and a plan to always think carefully needs to become the way you think *automatically*... Does that make sense?

Gandhi said, *"A man is the product of his thoughts; what he thinks, he becomes."* So you are a creator; you create with your every thought. You often create by default, *because you are getting what you are giving your attention to, wanted or unwanted!*

So mastery of thought is really a must in life. Do you understand?

However, you can become a master of the law of attraction without total life mastery, though freedom from pain, suffering and all of life's little 'nasties' may be worth your while when you're ready. When you are ready to end suffering, then the Bug Free Mind Process is ready for you too.

So How Do We Create?

Your brain is an organ of the conscious mind; it receives thoughts and, when your brain reasons those thoughts to be true, it is then brought into your reality. Your subconscious mind accepts the conclusions of your conscious mind, meaning you're in control, if you're in control of your thoughts.

Now, remember your conscious mind is only there when you are present. Most people are in fact in what I call *the waking sleep*, and so are not present very often. The waking sleep is when people are unconsciously awake and this, unfortunately, is how you are probably spending your life.

To tell if you are in the waking sleep, just consider if time seems to be passing faster each year. If it is, then you are becoming more and more unconscious as time is a constant. When you master control of your thoughts, you effectively slow down time as it stops getting faster and goes back to how much there was of it when you were a child.

But I digress… Your conscious mind is mostly filled with absolute garbage about how stuff works anyway, so it is very dysfunctional. Therefore, your subconscious mind is mostly fed on garbage which it believes to be true.

Why? Because you tell it it's true. So it is also accepting the conclusions of your garbage fed unconscious mind, which is why of course we create dysfunctional lives! Fix this and you fix the planet - that's everything by the way, as it is all just about identifying the problem! But we'll save fixing the planet for another time ;-)

Creating with our mind all starts with controlling our thoughts and, until we do that, we cannot create the life we desire. I'll cover a little on how to do that in the next chapter. You have to be able to control your mind, so that it can focus without interruption and without doubt on the thing that you do want.

If you continue to focus on what you do not 'want' (whatever that may be), then you will just create more of it. If you focus on wanting something then you will create more of wanting it and you will not get it. To be able to have something, you have to create the ability in your mind to have it before you have it, and to do that you have to be the one who controls your thoughts.

The secret is to then create what you desire with your thoughts, having attained a state of mind where you have actually had it happen and felt it happen in your mind, and in that process you become detached from it because you have already had it. Then what happens is you work diligently on making that a reality for everyone else, as it is already a reality in your mind. And you keep going until you get there.

Yes, that bit may need a bit of thought…

I slipped it in early, so you could leave if you think I'm wasting your time.

You create it, you have it, you detach from it, you work diligently on bringing it into the rest of our realities. That's the process described in words for the law of attraction. What you desire, your dream is created with just thought and then appropriate and obvious action.

How you make all that happen will take a little longer to explain, and making you a master of it will depend purely on your ability to control the thoughts in your head. So thoughts are kind of important, *all of them! Every last one!*

We are all creatures of creation, we create all of the time but the question is, creating what? The law of attraction is all just about you asking the right question and defining the answer whilst fully allowing it to happen at the right time and in the perfect way for you.

By now you should know… If you do not have what you desire, then you are not using the law of attraction properly.

For a few moments, observe how that makes you feel, as your observation will identify areas that you need to focus on. If you have no feelings, then stop speed reading and go back and read this again as *the challenge isn't to be the fastest reader, it is to get the greatest benefit.*

Ask yourself, *"Am I at ease with this moment?"* (Observe your feelings). Ask yourself often, *"What is going on inside me at the moment?"* Remember you should always be at least as interested with what you've got going on, on the inside as you are with what's happening outside.

To be able to create, you must not send out conflicting thoughts as this causes confusion, which is why you need to define and I mean DEFINE fully, exactly what you desire. Don't worry about doing it, as we are not quite there yet.

But, for now, just get your head round this; what you desire is already formed (the instant you desire it) and your job is to transform it into the physical world. As it is formed already, then your job is surely just *to allow it to come into your life.*

All creation happens in your mind, so you must become the observer of your thoughts… Remember, if you think you can control your thoughts then you can, if you think you can't then you can't… That is a choice… And also remember, no beating yourself up, *you should always be delighted with yourself*, as there is no benefit in not being delighted with yourself…

Chapter 3:

The Self-Made Illusion Holding Us Back

A few months before I had the epiphany that everyone was naturally successful, and in fact we are all designed to succeed, I got to see what the problem was which was holding most people back. I met the problem first hand as it was at the time holding me back too.

I cover this in detail in the first few chapters of Creating A Bug Free Mind, and you can get those chapters for free from the site www.ABugFreeMind.com so I'll keep it short and sweet here, as I strongly suggest you get those free chapters.

When we were children we didn't have the weight of bad influences, wrong assumptions and a mistrust of our own feelings holding us back. We also didn't have a voice in our head that sounded like us and kicked us about like a bully.

A by-product of our free thought is the entity we each allow to grow inside our minds, called our ego. It speaks, saying things to us like, *"You're not qualified to get the job, they'll find you out."* Or, *"Your friends don't like you, they think you're lying."* Or, *"Your husband doesn't love you."* Or, *"You're ugly."* If it's saying something nasty to you, it's not you, it's your ego!

Basically, as we age, this entity second guesses our every move and drives us to distraction. The voice sounds like us, so we think it is us. This entity's job is to keep us safe and it is made up of all your past experiences and the imagined horrible outcomes you've seen and heard about. Your ego then jumbles that lot together with life experiences from your parents and peers and delivers them back to you, *in an effort to stop you from making progress!*

Your ego sees progress as scary and so seeks to keep you safe, by keeping you trapped in the past which you have survived. So it knows that if you don't do anything new, then it will keep you safe. Unfortunately, we are creatures who are not satisfied with what we've had and want more, so internal conflict is inevitable.

So we begin to fight our ego and attempt to move forward. As we do, our ego throws even nastier things at us, to prevent us from moving. It'll tell us nasty things will happen to us, if we take a chance. That if we go into business, then we'll end up as homeless. If we try and love someone, that they will let us down! That we deserve to be depressed, as we are *such a bad person!*

Honestly, if this entity was a real person, you'd never go within a mile of them. But because we don't even notice the entity inside our own mind, because we think it's us, we then cannot control enough of our thoughts, to create progress. As little as a single thought taking us away from what we desire, can be enough to kill our dream... Can you see the importance of thought control now?

Our ego is allowed to live because we are not the controllers of our thoughts. We have what I call *chaotic thinking* going on inside our heads, and have no structure to stop the chaos and close our ego down.

Just imagine what society would be like, without the threat of the police and prison to keep us in order. This structure allows us to survive and live in a society. Without this structure, we would descend back into the dark ages relatively quickly. Basically, we need structure in our lives but no one has taught us we need structure in our thinking, too. Which is why 99% plus fail to get what they desire...

So why am I telling you about this little beastie and what's he or she got to do with the law of attraction and mastering it? As I covered earlier, this is how the law of attraction works:

To create what you desire with your thoughts, you have to have attained a state of mind where you have actually had it happen and felt it happen in your mind. And in that process you become detached from it because you have already had it. Then what happens is you work diligently on making that a reality for everyone else, as it is already a reality in your mind. And you keep going until you get there! This is how we create.

This is what happens in the minds of people who succeed with the law of attraction. All successful people have that process go on in their mind and life... But this doesn't just apply to amazingly successful people. We are all successful in different areas of our lives, plain and simple ordinary folk are every bit as good with this as the ultra-successful ones... Just in different areas.

And in the area we have been successful, then we applied the law of attraction correctly. In the areas we wish to succeed, then we are doing one or more bits of it wrongly.

An ultra-successful person may succeed in business, but not be able to succeed in a relationship with their husband or wife, or their children, whereas an ordinary person may struggle to succeed in the most basic business, or struggle to keep a job, but be fantastic in their relationships. We are all different. However, *the structure for success in ANY AREA is the same.* And therefore can be replicated by the person who masters the law of attraction.

So the law of attraction is just a process, it's a law and has rules. Play by them and it works, fail to play by them and it fails. So that is why *I know you can become a master of it!*

Now if you've tried to get the law of attraction to work before and have found that it doesn't, then you are doing one of more bits wrong. Here's an example of the law of attraction not working in the mind of someone trying to succeed in getting rich. We'll call him Ben. What I'm about to show you is just one of countless examples of how *chaotic thinking* screws up getting what you want from the law of attraction.

Ben says to himself, *"I'm going to use the law of attraction to get rich and bring me a million dollars by this time, next year."* Ben thinks he sets a desire with his thoughts but he has only come up with a vague, wishy washy, idea of what he wants. He has set no desire, as a desire needs to be somewhere you've been with your mind. None of us have been somewhere that was wishy washy...

Ben also has no idea that his subconscious mind is what goes and creates what he wants, when using the law of attraction. Or that it needs to know precisely what the result he wants is.

His subconscious mind has no idea what a million dollars is. His subconscious mind has been given the instruction that Ben wants a million dollars by next year. So his subconscious mind goes okay, let's give him that. And Ben gets more of wanting a million dollars by next year... He does not get the million dollars.

He can't get the million dollars as he has not had the million dollars in his mind. He hasn't gone and lived it having happened, he's not been there! ...And so his subconscious has no idea what it means.

Plus because he hasn't lived it, his ego says to him, *"that's never going to happen."* So Ben doubts he'll get the million. Now, when doubt comes in, it kills the dream dead. But Ben doesn't know that.

So Ben has heard that he must *try and think positively* to make this happen and says to himself, *"I believe I'm going to get this!"* To which Ben's ego says, *"No you don't, you know it's not going to happen. You're just kidding yourself, like you have in the past."* So Ben tries even harder to think positively and the ego continues to stick the boot in.

Ben has limited energy and persistence, his ego has limitless energy and knows its job is to keep Ben safe, so Ben's ego is very motivated to hold him back. After all, if Ben becomes rich, then his ego thinks that his friends will no longer like him...

Just so you know, ***trying to think positively will never work***. This requires massive sustained effort and is almost impossible when you have an ego chucking rocks at you every minute of every day.

But I've come off-track, I cover positive thinking in the right way in the Bug Free Mind Process. Ben's ego finds it easy to throw rocks at him, as there's chaos going on in Ben's attempt to create a million dollars, using the law of attraction.

Ben hasn't been specific about what he wants, he hasn't already had it in his mind, he doubts he's going to have it, he's fighting a war with his ego and not working on creating the million dollars... So what's he also doing wrong...?

Well he's still attached to it happening...

He needs it, he wants it still... Because he hasn't had it happen, there's no way he can detach from it, as that would go against what he wants and needs. The law's the law and, without detachment, the magic (the law) won't work.

So he's trying really hard but has missed a key ingredient and the law needs all ingredients. His desire hasn't happened in his reality, so he cannot detach from it and then just work on bringing it into everyone else's reality. It's not working and Ben has no idea why it's not, as he's *trying hard* to make it work.

He is attempting to manifest whilst attached and, like any law, it has rules. If you play by the rules, it works and if you don't, it doesn't. So now Ben's complete lack of detachment means he cannot do the last bit of the process correctly.

Ben's efforts are being used up in *trying to make it happen* and not *making it happen*. He cannot work diligently on making it happen, because he is working on trying to make it happen. He is trying too hard and as Yoda said, *"do or do not do; there is no try."*

Here, there is some real truth in the line Homer Simpson said, *"Trying in truth is the first step towards failure."* But, as usual, there are problems with word, as we have been taught we must try hard to succeed... But what if that is wrong and in fact that is a way **that guarantees failure**... Could that be why so many people fail and so few succeed?

Yet the ones who succeed, they try really hard, right? No, they are detached and just working diligently. You can call it trying, but they are not trying, they are doing. Only the unsuccessful keep trying... You may wish to consider that for a while ;-)

This brings up another point that you may also wish to consider... Words can be right and wrong. The same word can have multiple meanings and can be both good and bad. Words we use every day, and think are wonderful, can actually be disastrous words we should never even allow in our vocabulary...

For example, the word *hope* is universally loved, but is actually one of the most success destroying words in the world. I'm not going to come off track too much here but, as it's a little relevant to mastering the law of attraction, I'll cover just a bit on it.

Ben is *'hoping'* that his use of the law of attraction will succeed, as he dreads the thought of it not succeeding. But his subconscious mind sees him **hoping for something** (that's the instruction Ben's given his subconscious mind), so of course it delivers him **more hoping** next year, as our subconscious mind works to the law of attraction and gets Ben what it's instructed to get him…

He has instructed his subconscious mind, through *chaotic thought,* to give him *more hoping.* He's done that really well by accident. What he hasn't done well is instruct his subconscious mind to bring the million dollars. If he did that, then it would do that instead.

So, as the year passes by, Ben probably gave up on that desire many months before, as it took way too much effort (effort another bad thing when used in the wrong direction). So Ben failed on the last element of it, too; he didn't *keep going UNTIL he got there.*

And it is totally understandable why he quit on his journey. His journey was a nightmare, not a reward. When you apply the law of attraction correctly, then the Chinese proverb is true, *the journey becomes the reward.* But when you apply it wrongly, the journey is a frustrating nightmare and is frankly way too hard.

So Ben looks back and thanks to the help of his ego saying, *"see I told you this law of attraction stuff was just mumbo jumbo rubbish. It's not real, it's a con used by people to sell books. Why not go to the bar and have a few drinks as you deserve something, after all that effort you put I,'"* Ben thinks he said all of that and that was his conclusion, so goes off to the bar and tells the story of how the law of attraction doesn't work!

No, it's a law and therefore always works… The law of gravity doesn't stop working because we're using it wrongly. No, it's a law.

The funny thing is, or rather, the sad thing is, that his ego has sided against the law of attraction here, and yet after a few months, weeks or maybe only days of Ben's wallowing in his failure, his ego will say… *"You need to learn how to use the law of attraction, that's what you're doing wrong. You loser! Go and buy that book on it and have another go."*

Yes, your ego is a turncoat… So Ben, the puppet, buys another book, and gets his *'hopes'* up. Ben's ego says, *"Well done for taking action and making progress in life,"* which, of course, Ben hasn't actually done yet…

The book shows up and Ben's ego then says, *"You haven't got time to read that book… After all, it didn't work before. Go and have a beer, you deserve it."* A few weeks later, Ben's ego then says, *"See you bought that book and you haven't even looked at it. You're such a loser! Go and have a beer to feel better."* Ben thinks all of that was himself saying it to himself, but it wasn't.

Ben's ego has succeeded perfectly at keeping Ben trapped in the past and wallowing in self-pity. There is no chance that Ben's going to move forward now, is there? After all, Ben's ego has him in a great mind trap. It cracks the whip and makes him jump, by dangling the carrot of wanting a million dollars right in front of him. Then it sends him back to the bar, when he starts to make any progress.

Now do you see why I had to explain the little saboteur that's sitting inside our minds? Because, if we can see him or her, we can stop them! But **we cannot fix what we cannot see!**

How my dumb goal worked…

So, how did I get my dream of becoming a millionaire in two years to work, as my use of the law of attraction to create money looks on the surface, almost as dreadful as Ben's?

When I set the desire, I saw me in a few years time as the millionaire. I saw me living the lifestyle of someone rich. I did not see the toys. I felt the feeling, so lived and experienced how it would feel for me to be that millionaire. It felt really good. It felt right. It felt like I accomplished the prophecy my Great Uncle Dave had told me would happen.

I didn't doubt it at all, because I 100% knew he was right that I was destined to be a millionaire and that this would work, so I went there and was there. I set myself the goal of two years, because I thought that would be enough time to achieve it. This was daft as well, but I'll cover a little on time later and how irrelevant it is.

So I'd lived in my mind as the millionaire, it had happened in my reality. I felt the kudos of having achieved it. I felt the pride of being a millionaire, what I had wanted to be for as long as I could remember. So I had it happen in my mind. Then I became detached from needing it. I was still attached to having it happen, but it had already happened in my mind. So I'd had it! Now I was just bringing it into everyone else's reality, it felt right to make it happen, and essentially, **_it felt wrong to not make it happen!_** It was already a reality for me, after all.

I set about working diligently on my chosen route to creating the riches. I didn't need to think positively about achieving my dream, as *it felt right to make it happen*. So I just worked on it diligently. I loved the journey, the successful steps, the pitfalls… And although I didn't know it at the time, I kept going on it UNTIL it happened. As it happens, that turned out to be just over six months and added another million two weeks after that.

So was I smarter than Ben? No! I just used the tool we've all been given in the way it was designed to be used. I carved out the reality I had seen in my mind (I applied the rules of the law of attraction correctly).

Ben is using the chisel to carve out a hole in his foot and is dreading picking the chisel up again, as he's really bad with it. Then Ben is blaming the tool for his own lack of craftsmanship. *A bad workman blames his tools…*

So do you see now that, if I can get you to use the tool in the right way, with the right mind, then *it will be easy for you to become a master at the law of attraction?*

Consider this for a few seconds… Sure there's some obstacles to remove before you become the master craftsman but can you see how, if we remove the obstacles you previously couldn't see and use the tool in the right way, that you too can easily become a master?

Consider how you becoming the master will make you feel for a few seconds, or as long as you want to…

So everything in your life is a result of your previous and current thinking. Once you accept this as a fact, it can empower you to think better thoughts. *How do you feel about the truth in this now?*

Mastering the law of attraction is all about the details of the law. It's not one magic secret that fixes it. It's all about you understanding how the detail will trip you up, so you have to master that, in order to become the master you can so easily be.

I could tell you exactly how to use the tool right now but, if I do, then this is what will happen…

You'll learn it and ignore it, and probably doubt it. The truth is, it is easier to teach this to an untarnished child than it is to teach it to a worldly-worn adult, because your ego will pull apart all the work I do. So I have to build your mental muscles before you can take on and defeat your ego when manifesting… Is that okay with you?

Another problem is we are taught not to believe in some things and to doubt… whereas a child doesn't have this baggage, so they'll accept it as the truth without plenty of evidence. If you're anything like I was in my early 30's, and always looking for the catch, then you'll doubt this will work and therefore you'll be right… So first I have to get you past your doubt too, so that you can master the law of attraction… Is that okay with you?

A still mind...

Lao Tzu said, *"To the mind that is still, the whole universe surrenders."* So we've got to give you a structured thinking technique, to help you still your mind and begin silencing your mind. This is you taking back control on demand.

In areas of your life that you succeed at, you will already do this without thought. For the areas you struggle to succeed, we need some structure and then, after a while, it'll be as automatic as it is in the successful areas. So this may feel a little awkward to begin with but this is just you reshaping your mind using brain plasticity... I suggest you decide to just go with it and see what happens.

When you practise silencing your mind, at some point you attain no-mind; that is when you literally think of nothing. No thoughts of any kind - the Zen people call this 'Satori' but that's far too clever for me, so I'll stick with *'no mind.'* This does not mean you are asleep or in a trance; no, you are just fully present, fully alert and fully aware.

You will probably have experienced glimpses of this throughout your life and they have passed probably without much notice. However, the technique of silencing the mind's chatter, together with some other techniques which I am about to show you, will create the by-product of *no mind* in the same way as continued practise of the martial arts creates the by-product of Chi.

This *no mind* isn't something you have to be super-human to get, either; all it is, is you switching your thinking off. I have taught both my children to do this, so you can learn it too; admittedly, they didn't have as much insane chatter going on as we adults but there is still junk in their minds.

When you decide you are going to bring in *no mind*, don't try, just bring it in and silence your mind. I suggest you find your favourite spot in the house and that it is very quiet when you first do this, so that there are no external distractions.

Once you do it, see how long you can hold it for. I play a game with David, practising how fast you can bring it in and how long you can hold it for. It takes him a few seconds to silence his mind before bringing it in and he can usually hold it for about a minute, which is of course fine.

In fact, the power of this is so great that once you can control it and bring it in on demand anywhere, you only need to hold it for a few moments to completely regain control and effectively restart your mind, and have crystal clear thinking.

I practised bringing in *no mind* in all sorts of conditions; on the train, in the car, in shops, in a bar, while playing music, while playing heavy metal music. I kept practising and, in the end, there was no place that I could not still my mind in an instant. Now I haven't kept this up to that level, as I just don't need that level, but I trained hard enough so that I could actually do that.

No mind will just happen when you are ready. Don't struggle with it, and don't force it, just allow it to happen when you feel you would like to be able to.

I suggest you keep returning to this piece, as if you get this, and can turn it on whenever you want to, then you cannot not notice the immediate change in your reality. This hidden obstacle will never be invisible again. Spend plenty of time building your foundation; you can't put the roof on a house, until you have built the walls and your walls need to have a solid foundation…

Side note: – *I have mentioned repetition already, but repetition is a master skill. People complain when I repeat things, but the skill of repetition is essential to learn. It is not the things we are yet to discover that will change our lives, but the things we have learnt and ignored. Through repeating great stuff, you will acquire great power, so do not be afraid to re-read a good book instead of reading a new book. You are not missing out; in fact you've already missed out, so it is time to go back and re-read.*

If you struggle with the simplicity of just deciding to have a silent mind and hold it for a period of time. Then there are several techniques to help attain this, which I share for free in the first few chapters of Creating A Bug Free Mind. You can access them on www.ABugFreeMind.com.

One thing I will say on *no mind* before I leave it for this work….

I consider silencing the mind to be the foundation skill to achieving anything you desire in life. In my Bug Free Mind Process, I get people to return back to mastering *no mind* again and again, until they master it.

I am not a person who meditates in the conventional way. I always saw it as taking up way too much time. However, I wanted the result that being a master of meditating would give me so, as I'm a very lazy person, I found a way through no-mind to get the benefit within a few seconds.

If you are into meditating then you may find this hard to believe, so don't believe me. Go and give it a go and see for yourself. If you're not into meditating, then trust me that this tiny little amount will be of unlimited value to you, so is well worth your time mastering it.

Consider this. It's pretty difficult to master the law of attraction, if you're living in *the waking sleep*, so being able to silence your mind, and become very present, wakes you up and allows you to use the full focus of your mind's power.

Your Thoughts Are Not Static

Before I leave this section, there's one more structured thought I need to give you for control of your own mind.

We think we are standing still but we are on a world that is spinning very fast, that is also travelling around the Sun at phenomenal speed and which is also spinning around the galaxy at incomprehensible velocity. And it goes on...

When you actually begin to look at how the universe works, both on a massive scale and on a micro scale, you find that **NOTHING STANDS STILL**...

The same is true of your thoughts; your thoughts either *help you* and take you towards your dreams and desires, or they *hurt you* and take you away from your dreams and desires. So *no thought stands still!*

Now don't underestimate the power that this one little thought structure can bring to your life because, when you master it, you obtain the power of *only being able to think thoughts, which help you!*

Can you imagine how easy it is for me to make the law of attraction work, as I only think things which help me? Thoughts which harm me have been trained to either never be there, or if they come up, are noticed and seen as useless and destructive as they are clearly taking me away from my dreams... As soon as they are noticed, they dissolve without any effort.

Imagine that, *all the things that harm you dissolving in an effortless way...* Does that sound good?

So consider these thoughts for a few seconds and notice and feel the direction they can take you...

"I don't deserve to be rich?" - *"I deserve to be rich."*

"I don't deserve to be loved." - *"I deserve to be loved."*

"I feel good." - *"I feel bad."*

"I love my life." - *"I hate my life."*

It was easy, right? One thought goes the wrong way and one goes the right way. But because you have not been trained to notice them, you allow thoughts that hurt you into your mind...

Consider this, do you think it will be easier to succeed with only thoughts that help, or with allowing thoughts that harm into your mind to mix in with the good ones and cause confusion? Is it easy to see why things go wrong, when you allow negative thinking in?

Because you are the one who has control of your mind. With structure to your thinking, you can now choose to not allow bad thoughts to remain. *If you choose to use the technique.* And as I've said, it only takes one thought going the wrong way to kill a dream.

I'm not going to cover any more on negativity here; it's covered in A Bug Free Mind, if you want to remove every shred of it from your life. But all you need to master the law of attraction is to understand, and then practise, *not allowing any negative thinking at all,* regarding what you wish to manifest.

Aristotle said, *"The aim of the wise is not to secure pleasure but to avoid pain."* By you avoiding the pain of negative thinking, you automatically, without any effort, secure pleasure in getting what you want.

The work you must do is not to think positively about getting what you want, but work diligently on the removal of all doubt that you will get what you want.

One more thing to understand is that *your thoughts cause your feelings.*

Without structured thought, your feelings are created by *accidental* or *chaotic thought.* But once you apply simple structure as I've shown you above, if you want happiness, you have happiness. If you want love, you have love. You have the power to control all of this and *all* your feelings.

Now if you think you can, then you're right, if you think you can't, then you're right, too. As you are the architect, you are either controlling on purpose, or allowing your ego to control by accident... This chapter gives you the power of choice. Previously, you had the illusion of choice...

So now you can begin feeling whatever you want, even if it's not there yet, as you are the person who decides what thoughts go on in your head.

But before we leave this, let's look just a little deeper at *the power of structured thinking v chaotic thinking.*

Chapter 4:

Structured Thinking v Accidental (Chaotic) Thinking

Consider this; who teaches us to think? Who teaches us how to think? Who taught _YOU how to think?_

No one!

They all just taught you **what to think.**

Think about it: Thou shalt not steal – _what to think._ Don't touch that – _what to think._ Think positively – _what to think._

Think about the advice you had from your parents and your friends, from the TV, growing up and even now… **You should be afraid** – _what to think._ **You should be worried** – _what to think._

If you study personal development work, then you will find when you look, that they all teach you _what to think_ and unknowingly _assume you know,_ as the teacher does, _how to think._

I realised that the successful knew _how to think_ instinctively, so they didn't see the need to teach it. They knew _what to think_ as they saw the application of that as their route to success. For example, don't think negatively, think positively - _what to think._

Now when I decided to write on personal development, one thing I wanted to do was to share something new which had never been shared before and so I saw this as the missing piece in personal development, and in teaching in general.

So if I do teach any _what to think_ information, I then back it up with _how to think._ But mainly I teach _how to think_, as that's all you need to apply and get results.

For example, I've had the pleasure of teaching my children _how to think_, not _what to think_. I give them freedom to think what they want, so I do not restrict them and do not have many of the parental hardships which a lot of parents go through – thus making my life much easier… I like easy, I don't like hard! So I work on prevention rather than cure.

I give them _the ability to think accurately about anything._ So they excel at school and find it easy to pass exams when others find it hard and painful. I've taught them how to enjoy exams, so they enjoy them.

Bear in mind when I say this, that both my wife and I were 'C' grade students. My children are both 'A' grade students. I've taught them *how to think*, so they succeed at all they *choose*, or *have* to do. I've shown them how to avoid pain and, when they do that, all that remains is pleasure and success.

My son is in the gifted and talented section of the school, where the *'really naturally gifted kids are.'* He said to me recently that he didn't deserve to be there, as they were using words he didn't even understand. He's right, they are way cleverer than him!

He'd got there by getting a pass rate in exams that showed he was at that level. But, in truth, he wasn't, he just has the advantage over all other children of knowing *how to think*, meaning *he can critically think about everything and control his emotions with ease...*

Both my children are the leaders of their peer groups. Other children are drawn to them, because they exude confidence and security. They do this automatically, because they have structure to their thinking.

What they *choose to think* is entirely up to them. I do not have to consider most of the worries parents do because, when faced with situations, they have their logical, structured, thinking ready to go to work for them.

For example, my son David is in an environment where drugs are everywhere. But it is illogical for him to participate as he sees the benefit, *the high*, and sees the cost, *the low*. So he is free to choose what's logical, without peer pressure getting a foothold. His thinking shows him that the highs may be nice, but the lows are nasty...

So, on balance, it's obvious to avoid the whole situation, as any of you who have never used drugs, or have used them and then stopped, realised after time. Eventually, structured thinking worked. So I just gave it to them before, meaning they didn't have to go on the journey, as they could do it in their mind instead.

This among several other reasons is why we were asked by a country to give a proposal for putting the full A Bug Free Mind Process into its entire education system. It's early days still here but, since they asked, four other countries have expressed an interest too. So you don't want to underestimate the power of learning *how to think*.

Later on, I'll share the story of how I used the law of attraction to get a country to ask me to put my system for structured thinking into their education system.

The wonderful truth is that *there's no limit to how much better you can think.* You just have to become *a master at structuring your thinking so that you always think the right way, instead of accidentally thinking the wrong way.*

With structured thinking, you don't really have emotional problems. But if they come up, they are dealt with or enjoyed.

I'm sure you've been told already that you can change your emotion immediately, by thinking of something joyful, or singing a song, or remembering a happy experience. But just imagine if you didn't have to try hard, that you could control everything nasty without any effort at all… *Would that be good? What do you think the benefit of that would be to your life?*

Just imagine that for a few seconds, no more fear, no more worry… Two of the biggest dream killers gone… *How will that feel?*

Buddha said, *"All that we are is a result of what we have thought"* So spending a little time mastering some simple structured thinking will result in you getting a lot more results in exactly the same way as my children do. And in the same way as my A Bug Free Mind students do. I'll share some very cool proof of the results later.

However, if you leave your thinking to happen accidentally without structure, just with *what to think* information… then chaos reigns and people can often find themselves trapped in a real life soap opera. As without structure, how do you stop the mess from happening?

So once you become aware and then fully understand the effect that *accidental chaotic thinking* has on your life, it becomes obvious that you've found the solution to the problem.

I trust I've gone deep enough here to explain the benefits of structuring your thinking to master the law of attraction at least. And I trust I've given you a clear explanation of why the law of attraction may have appeared not to work for you, or others you know, in the past.

Right, let's now give you something that will really make you think…

Chapter 5:

How What We Know May Not Be So...

Have you heard this about the law of attraction before...?

Decide what you want ... Believe you can have it ... Believe you deserve it ... Believe it's possible for you. We have been told to do that and we can master the law of attraction... So what's wrong with you, surely all you need is the answer right?

Can you see that the teaching here is more *what to think*... Our complex minds can't actually 'believe' that. So it isn't the answer. And we have the problem that the words I'm writing here are not our natural language; our natural language is feelings and intuition. At best, words are a poor form of communication.

So knowing the answer doesn't get you the result... You may want to stop and really consider this at length, as it's of paramount importance when it comes to getting results in life. So I'll say it again, knowing the answer will probably not and, in fact, will likely not, get you the result...

Don't believe me, then I'll prove it to you.

You do know you should only eat whole foods that are healthy for you and help you lead a full life, right? Sure you do; we all do.

You do know you should exercise regularly to stay healthy and live a long life, don't you? Sure you do; we all do.

You do know you shouldn't get angry and stressed, as it doesn't help you and is bad for your health, right? Sure you do; we all do... (Anger and stress are a choice too, which I fix in A Bug Free Mind).

You do know you should be happy and grateful, yes? Sure you do; we all do...

...**We all know all that stuff, *right?***

Do you get it? *We all know things, which we don't actually know!*

Because we don't truly know something until we are living it as *a way of life*. The word *know* is used to cover the time between when we don't really *know*, but say we do and when we do actually *know* (and a couple of *'sort of know'* stages in-between.)

25

I'll explain this a bit more shortly but, first, I want to show you just how powerful you already are when you *really do know something for sure...*

Reality Is Negotiable

Albert Einstein told us that, *"Reality is merely an illusion, albeit a very persistent one."* What that means to you and I and anyone wishing to control things using the law of attraction... is that this illusion, which looks real, is just an illusion that can be changed and shaped to suit us!

Anyone who has studied the law of attraction will have heard this sort of thing before: -

"You are a living magnet, you attract into your life situations and circumstances that are in harmony with your dominant thoughts". Sounds really good, doesn't it?

If you're in the personal development/self help world, then this sounds like a *'good plan'.* Well there's loads of good stuff in this but it is written in the wrong way to make it applicable and therefore not much use to aid you in actually going and creating. Here's somewhat of an improvement: -

"You are a creator; you create, in your life, situations and circumstances which are in harmony with your dominant thoughts."

It hasn't got the same Hollywood flare; however, it is far more accurate and applicable. Absorb that into your subconscious and you'll see what difference it makes.

So use this to apply the law of attraction fast; simply decide what you desire and it is now created (that was hard!). It is now... and was already there, of course... Okay, we just stepped a little off the map. I'll explain that a bit more, shortly.

After creating it by desiring it, then you live in the grateful way you would do, after having already had your desire come into your life. You just spend the vast majority of your time taking steps to now aid bringing this into your physical reality, whilst all of the time doing so without any attachment to the end result!

When you then go about your life, you must be open to coincidences 'just happening'. Your ego may work on doubting that they were you manifesting. That's okay, it can doubt what it chooses to doubt, and you can think what you choose to think... So keep your eyes open, as you are the creator.

Though it does sound too easy, doesn't it? *"Hey Andy, this don't work!"* Well that is how we have all ALREADY used the law of attraction in our lives when we apply it as a way of life, rather than attempting to 'believe' in it. So, in fact, you have already done it this way!!!

Now you may choose to spend some time on thinking about what you have that is good and what you have that is bad in your life right now, or in the past. Why not see if you can trace the creation of the good or the bad, back to the time when you first *thought it into existence!* Then go back and see what you did next, what steps you unconsciously took to *bring it into your physical reality.*

When you do find evidence, go back to the time you created it. Feel the emotions which were present when you first created it and figure out how you *'knew'* it would happen. These are the times when you have used this wonderful tool before and you did so without *knowing,* just as *a way of life.*

Now all my job is, is to get you to replicate what you've done before but, this time, *have you notice* exactly how you did it! The easiest way to get you to use the law of attraction properly going forward is to show you how you already used it so masterfully in your past.

The law doesn't care how it is used, it has no emotions, it does not care if you 'believe' in it or not. For this, I am going to have to touch on quantum physics but if you're interested I go a lot deeper into quantum physics in Using A Bug Free Mind, which is part 2 of the Process.

So a little quantum physics… What you think about literally becomes real now. I'm not talking about, *ooh I'm thinking of pink sea lions in full scuba gear dancing on the top of clouds, therefore, where are they?* I'm thinking of things which I create and other people create too, some of these are big and some small… you know, *everything in our lives.*

There was a guy working on the trains, in Russia I think. His job was to clean out the refrigeration trains. These were sealed cars once the doors shut and, after approximately ninety minutes, the air would all be used up if the door was closed. Or the cold would freeze a person in a similar amount of time. It was a job, which required the cleaner to latch the door open so that, if for some reason the carriage moved, the door would not slam shut.

Well, apparently, on this occasion, the carriage moved and the cleaner had not latched the door, so the door slammed shut. The cleaner *knew* he only had only ninety minutes of air before he would suffocate or freeze to death. As there weren't many people around and he wasn't expected back for a while, he *knew* the chances of someone finding him in time were slim. He must have made as much noise as he could and he tried everything to get the doors open, but no one found him for some time. When they opened the door he was dead. It was later found that he had frozen to death.

27

A guy died, so what has this got to do with the law of attraction? Well, quite a lot actually as he had, in my opinion, had this nightmare happen plenty of times in his dreams (that is a pure guess based on my study of people). You can visualise bad, just as you can visualise good.

But this is far stranger than that and here's why it really has something to do with the law of attraction. The vent was open on the carriage and the freezer car was not sealed. The air didn't run out and the temperature was normal… *so how did he die?*

The conclusion of the coroner was that he 'believed' so strongly that *he was freezing* that for him, **he created this into his reality and he froze to death!** He used his own mind to kill himself – this is how powerful your mind is and it can be used to create or un-create.

Yes I know… this is some story… and goes towards explaining how we really do think things into existence and how Einstein was right, *reality really is negotiable.*

But why do we think we know things when we don't actually apply them?

This fascinated me… Why couldn't I keep applying things I learnt and knew 100% would work and would help me? I had to find the answer, as I wanted to know!

Mark Twain said, *"It ain't what you don't know that gets you into trouble. It's what you know for sure that just ain't so."* The answer came down to the simplest of things… *We don't know what we think we know…*

The word ***know*** and the mind state behind it changes everything…

It turns out there are at least four levels of *knowing something* and unless you get to the fourth and highest level of *know*, then your success is, at best, highly unlikely.

The first level of knowing something - When we learn something, we think we *know* it but this is only the intellectual and weakest level of *knowing something*. This is where most people end their studying, as our ego is very quick to halt our progress at this point by telling us to reward ourselves, as we now *know something* more and have made progress!

No, we've just learnt something. We haven't made any real progress at this point, we are just intellectually a bit more clever. And, in truth, as my students will know, I often speak about the addition of knowledge without application of the knowledge, as *being destructive, not constructive!* But our ego likes knowledge as it uses it to trap us.

For example, let's take someone who *knows* they should be eating healthily, as they are at high risk of getting a disease.

A doctor comes on the TV and says, *"You should be eating an apple a day, as it keeps the doctor away."* Our ego then pipes up, *"Well, I know that!"* So we instantly dismiss the doctor's comment and carry on with our day. We do this unconsciously, as we're in the waking sleep almost always when we say *we know something, without thought of whether or not we are applying it.*

Now, we didn't notice that even though we **know** we should eat an apple a day, that we weren't eating an apple a week, let alone a day… That didn't come out, as the word **know** swept the wisdom under the carpet before it could be useful.

So we don't **know** what we think we **know**… *Knowing things* can actually be much more destructive to our lives than *not knowing things*, which is a version of what Mark Twain meant.

Consider if you will the same scenario of a person being ill and looking for a potential cure and the doctor says the same line. The person *not knowing* that an apple a day could help them would probably give this new wisdom a try, as they are looking for a cure and are not hindered by *knowing something* which they don't actually *know*.

I told you this would make you think ;-)

The second level of knowing something – This is the *understanding level*, which is above *know*, where you feel this is *what must be happening*, but you are still not living it yet. When you get to this level, you've been a fairly persistent studier, though your ego will be doing it's best to keep you from applying what you *know*.

The third level of knowing something – This is the living it level… Now this is a very high level of *know*, it's where you live it in your life…. and only a very tiny percentage of people get to this level…

But this is not even the highest level of *know* and this is a very dangerous level of *know* too, because you *know* so much that you can utterly convince yourself that you do *know* it…

But you don't, as there's still one more level of *know* to go…

The fourth level of knowing something – When it has become *a way of life*…

This is when you live it as *a way of life*... This is the very highest level and it is the level required for success in any and all areas of life. Less than 1% of people usually make it to this level in virtually anything.

This is when *you no longer think you know it,* as you are well past that... It is now at your core. You do not need to consider it, because it is now *your way of life.*

As an example, I left *knowing* the law of attraction exists behind a long time ago. I just live it now. Every thought in my mind has to be helpful and in the pursuit of giving me a wonderful experience or building me my dreams; this is *my way of life.*

People wonder why they cannot succeed and it is because they have to take their level of *knowing something* from the intellectual level right up to the highest level and make it their *way of life.*

You attained this level of *knowing* for anything you succeeded at... and so did every other successful person out there.

But this level of *know* unfortunately has its own weakness, as nothing is static in this world and life can get in the way... This is why people can succeed and then not make it back. Because they lost this level of know...

So that means that to *know* something is probably even at this level only temporary... Yet we casually throw the word *know* around in our daily language and have no idea that what *we know* we *know,* may not even be so, and ...is only temporary at best ...unless it is maintained...

I've attained this level of *know* about a lot of things in life, and I've lost this level of *know* more than once! The reason the whole Bug Free Mind Process was created was to help me make sure *I never lost it again*... But that can only ever be work in progress as our minds are not static...

The trouble is our egos like to tell us that we can learn something and *know it* and so have it and not need to consider it again... And we like that... It's an easy sale, because when it comes to *knowing stuff,* we are real pigeons!

I found I was being conned by myself where it came to *knowing something* and so I needed a way to ensure that I remained at the *highest level of knowing* when it came to mindset and success... I needed something that made this *way of life* simple...

So I decided to create my Success Made Simple videos which is basically the Bug Free Mind Process converted into a video course and broken down into tiny bite-sized blocks of wisdom.

I did this so that I'd have to work on my mind whilst building the course. I thought it was an 18-month project and I am happy to say I underestimated the task... I've already had two very happy years building this *way of life* series and I expect there to be another two years still to go...

This work has allowed me to keep my mind at the highest level of *know* there is...

It is not like a normal course as there is no end. People who do it are not studying to get to the end of the course, they are studying to attain or maintain the highest level of *knowing something*... It's like a healthy life plan for your mind.

So what you want to do is start to notice when you say you *know something* that you are not doing. Because *you cannot fix what you cannot see.* So we first have to notice and then, through the act of noticing, we start shifting the brain about a bit, as this act changes our thinking, which in turn changes our results...

Okay, let's go deeper now on how exactly to have something before you have it...

Chapter 6:

You Have To Have It Before You Can Have It

I've spoken already about the importance of your life being in harmony with your dominant thoughts. Well, what I want to do in this section is explain it in a way where you don't just know that, as I just proved to you that *knowing* it is useless and probably destructive.

What I want to do is explain it here in a way that makes it easy for you to live *a way of life* that is this: *"You being the creator; you are creating in your life situations and circumstances which are in harmony with your dominant thoughts."* So you and I take you from knowing it to beginning to live to it. Does that sound good?

Albert Einstein said, *"Imagination is everything. It is the preview of life's coming attractions."* What you imagine will be your future. But it has to be a complete upload... What I mean by that is...

You've seen the movies where they are trying to download or upload some software and if it doesn't make it to 100% it completely fails yes? Well you have to upload your dream until it's uploaded 100%. Thinking positively about it happening for a while won't cut it. This has to be something which is done, finished, uploaded.

When you get the hang of this skill, before you know it, you will KNOW you are the creator, you will KNOW you can create anything and you will KNOW it so much that it will become *your way of life*. So we have to have it before we can have it.

The first choice you have to make for this is to <u>be happy</u>.

Have you heard that you will not be happy when you get there, that you have to be happy first? Maybe you've never heard this before, or is this something you've learnt and dismissed? Or is this something you know to be true and have dismissed. Or is this something you live as *a way of life*?

Happiness can mean a lot of different things to people. I, for example, don't ever get ecstatically happy which may or may not be your definition of happiness. But I can see something wonderful happen and tears will roll down my face. And then at times I can be really happy though sound really grumpy. So happiness can be a wide range for me. But the state of happiness is a choice and must be chosen from where you are now.

In 2009, a couple of months before I lost tens of millions and I had a LOT of unhappy creditors and a MASSIVE amount of problems that were frankly insurmountable. Plus COUNTLESS people who had lost their mentor and were feeling really low and lost. And at the time I had no income and no idea exactly what I was going to do to create one.

It was not a good time, to say the least, to be me. I really could've been in the worst mindset state of my life. But I wasn't. Instead, I was happy and not just happy. I was in the most serene and wonderful mindset state I have ever been in my life. I was so happy and serene that all my friends thought I'd lost it.

In fact it was only the fact that my wife Alison, who was there to witness it, was able to tell people that I was fine and there wasn't a problem with me. As my state of mind was so extraordinary, that it was in no way normal to other people. As most people think you can only be happy if there's good things going on in your life to be happy about.

Now scoot forward to today. I am rich again and financially free to do as I choose. I've got more options and alternative directions to go in business than I've ever had and my work is fun in all directions. I've designed my life to suit everything I want. Every day, I change the lives of more people than I've ever reached before. Frankly, I've achieved more in five years than most people achieve in a lifetime and I'm still happy. But I'm not *as happy* as I was when it was all going wrong.

On the surface, this doesn't make sense but, if you look deeper, you'll see I was living to the truth that what had happened had happened and I would deal with that as I could. But I wouldn't let that affect my future.

I was living *as the creator; creating in my life situations and circumstances which were in harmony with my dominant thoughts."* I switched my mind into a *way of life,* which created the future I desired. And for that to occur, I had to be happy (actually in real life happy with my life then in that horrible situation) **IF** I wanted everlasting happiness. So, if I could do it with all that going on, then I think you can do it from where you are too.

And before you say you can't, let me tell you about an old woman I saw interviewed on the TV regarding her experiences in the Holocaust. The interviewer turned to her and asked how she did it. How could she survive every day in the death camps, knowing that each day could be her last? Without missing a beat the old woman said, *"There was always something funny going on in the camp."* What an amazing and abnormal mindset!

That woman, who was probably in her twenties when that horror happened, chose to see what was happening as humorous… She chose happiness over any of the horrible useless emotions she could've easily allowed to happen. She survived and had a wonderful life thanks, to her ability to choose what happens in her head. So if she can do it, then so can you too.

Consider for a few seconds, can you choose to be happy where you are now? If you cannot choose it easily yet, then use this thought structure to choose it... *'I choose to be happy now.' 'I choose to feel good now.'*

Try them right now and notice how you feel when you say them. When you find you are not happy, use them.

When you find yourself low and unhappy, remember that you will not, and probably cannot, be happy when you get there... You have to be happy now, so choose to be happy now. Learn this, and apply this, and pretty soon you will be happy. That tiny thought structure made it easy for me to be happy in a very horrible situation. So all you have to do is use it.

The first choice you have to make is to be happy with where you are, which you can now do, as long as you don't do the silly thing of knowing it before you start to live it. As you live it, then it will turn into *a way of life* fairly quickly.

Now the next choice you have to make is gratitude.

You've probably heard this before and know you need this too, just like you do with eating the apple a day. But now you've got to take this from knowing it (which is useless) to living it, so that it becomes *a way of life*.

This is simple to achieve. Take out a pen and notepad and write down a list of what you've had happen in your life that you were grateful for. The experiences. The relationships. They can have ended badly too if you are running short on ideas. But I'm talking about the wonderful moments in relationships. Or just choose wonderful happy moments.

The moment you got married, the moment your child was born, the moment you passed an exam, the way you laughed one day... These can be anything you are grateful for. When I wrote my list I scribbled down 79 things without letting up. If I wrote it today there would be hundreds more moments, if not thousands more, which I am grateful for. But with just, say, 10 to 15 moment, you have a list.

All you do next daily and until you enter *living life in a grateful way,* which may take a few days or a few years is, you read your list to yourself. *Complex stuff right?*

Take the first moment and go and experience it again FULLY! Be there! Enjoy how wonderful the moment was again. If you want to cry, cry. Be happy and love it. Then after a minute or so, read the next one and be there too.

Choose to pick them randomly from the list if you want. Or read them out in an order... It doesn't matter. But I'd suggest spending at least 15 minutes a day building *a grateful way of life.*

This technique does a stack more good for your life too, as I explain in Creating A Bug Free Mind. All you need to know to become the master of the law of attraction is that you must demonstrate to your subconscious mind what you are grateful for.

In doing this, you are then communicating with it and saying, *"Look I love this, please give me more of loving this sort of thing."* Your subconscious mind being the perfect servant to you will then give you more to be grateful for.

Now for a second think about this…

When you wallow in self pity and doubt your success, you are communicating with your subconscious mind and saying, *"Look, please give me more of this! I obviously love it as I wouldn't be torturing myself otherwise."* Your subconscious mind, which has no powers of deduction at all, just decides, *"Okay, I'll send you more to feel sorry about."*

So gratitude will bring more into your life immediately! Do you understand how much just this can alter your experience of life?

If you have a nasty thing you have to do each day, like being stuck travelling somewhere regularly, then imagine if you chose to consider your grateful list whilst you're doing the thing you don't like.

Without any effort, the thing you don't like will not matter anymore, as you will be very happy and even grateful that the nasty thing was there, as it gave you the opportunity to consider what you have to be grateful for… Consider it… You can switch off the bad things in life just by changing your thinking at the right time and in the right way.

But also consider this, *do you see how knowing this can now be destructive too, unless you start applying it…* How do you feel about knowing this and maybe not applying it…

The next choice is to give up worrying about time…

I talk about rushing, and being busy, and working hard, in the Bug Free Mind Process and mastery over them all is relevant for living a wonderful life. But, for mastering the law of attraction, you just have to decide to give up worrying about time.

As humans, we are the worrying animal. No other creature on Earth worries, we invented this 'dis-ease'. But I wasn't like everyone else, as I didn't worry. I always saw worrying as something that we could choose to do.

Everyone, and I mean everyone, told me I was wrong and that I should worry. No, that is herd mentality, caused by everybody doing something wrong and therefore us seeing it as normal. We can look at something potentially bad happening and choose to worry or not. We don't have to and, in fact, should not worry, as it's pointless!

So the first truth you have to accept is that you have a choice about worrying in all areas of life. All I'm covering here is time, so if you want the rest, then you can go and get the full A Bug Free Mind Process .

Think about time for a second, we see time as if it's running out and so we feel we must rush. We feel we must rush because we are told to by all the other people rushing, that we must do that, or we will fail to get what we want... Well consider, the world (the herd) has a 99% plus failure rate at getting what they want, so maybe it's time for you to go in a different and more pleasurable direction... What do you think?

I see that there will always be enough time, so I always have enough time... It's about demonstrating abundance by living abundantly. Their way of doing things doesn't work. I do not rush, I just work diligently and the work will get done when it gets done. We only worry about time when we self impose deadlines on ourselves.

If you imagine and choose to start to live to the fact that *everything will always work out for the best for you*, then you can stop worrying about time. Because whatever happens will be for the best! If you fail to do something, then that is the best, if you succeed to do something, then that is the best... *Simple, but not too simple, I trust?*

I live thinking that everything will always work out for the best. That's everything! If something goes wrong and looks bad, my default thinking is, *"I wonder how this is going to work out for the best."* Then I just consider it, and carry on with my life.

Sure enough, even the most horrible things end up being for the best... ALLWAYS! This is because I think they will, so they do. If you think they won't, then you'll be right, too.

A choice! And choice is the problem, as if I could just instruct you to think this way, then your life would be automatically better from now on. But as you have a choice over this, then you can choose to not think like that and so it won't be automatically better. Without choice, the pain would go away! You may wish to spend a while pondering on this, as it'll move the neurons around in your mind quite a lot...

So by choosing to know it always works out for the best, then you have the ability to learn the lessons life gives you, so that you can move on. If you've ever felt stuck, then it is simply because you are failing to learn a lesson life is attempting to teach you.

Your ego will probably be telling you that I'm talking sh*t right now, as a particular event from your life was **ALL bad!** So, as the ego has been kind enough to attempt to halt your progress here thanks to a previously bad experience, why don't you now go and choose to look at how that bad experience either turned out to be a good thing, or if the good result hasn't shown itself yet, then consider how it *could* turn out to be a good thing…

Take a few moments now and teach yourself the life lesson that *it always is going to work out for the best for you.*

Okay, as you go about your days, now *choose to know it's going to work out for the best* and it will. Watch the bad event come up and consider what life is attempting to teach you. The more you live thinking this way, the more you give up considering time and worrying about time as you are *now* just living *now.* You are not rushing to get there as you are there, you are enjoying the journey and are being grateful for all the lessons life is giving you… You are becoming the magnet and attracting or creating the change in life you desire, and have designed, using the law of attraction.

So do you think you can remember to apply that thought structure, *"Everything is always going to work out for the best for me… So how is what's just happened going to help me, what do I need to learn?"* Then just relax and consider… Whilst carrying on with your life.

Another truth about time is that time ceases to matter when you know you are going to get there. You will see this truth happen when we go through mastering the law of attraction near the end of this short book.

And the other truth is this; *everything happens at the right time and in the right way.* Consider this; if you think like that, then you remove the worry of time from your life as, if it hasn't happened yet, then it wasn't meant to, as everything works out best for you. Do this and you are applying one of the most wonderful laws of all, the law of least effort. I explain that and all its wonderful benefits in the Bug Free Mind Process too.

So do I walk this talk…

Whilst I was building my new fortune, at times I thought I'd make a breakthrough at a certain point… and time after time it didn't happen. The first time it didn't happen, I thought it should have done.

But then I relaxed and considered why it hadn't happened. I reminded myself that everything always works out the best for me, and that everything happens at the right time and in the right way... So what lesson had I failed to learn? Or maybe it wasn't meant to work out when I thought it was... So I went back to just working diligently on bringing my reality into everyone else's.

Sure enough the riches came again at the right time and in the right way. They happened because there were lessons I still needed to learn before they showed up. So I looked for the lessons, found them, learnt them, lived them and then sure enough the success I designed occurred. Plus wonderful things needed time to happen too so, because I didn't attempt to force things but allowed the design to unfold, then things worked easily.

All that was different was the timescale. However, the success I designed ended up being far bigger than I imagined and in a much shorter time for the bigger stuff than I considered was even possible. I allowed this to happen because I was open to a greater manifestation than I'd designed. I'll tell this story later on.

The secret is by giving up on time; you allow your subconscious mind to deliver the result you asked for in your creation. So I suggest you spend time considering giving up worrying about time though, as always, it's your choice if you do or not...

If you turn it over to the universe, you will be surprised and dazzled by what is delivered... This is where magic and miracles happen.

So you are happy, grateful and not worried about time. As you are living to the truth that everything will work out for you at the right time and in the right way...

Can you see how just these few tiny changes will alter your very experience of life? How will that make you feel?

What you'll have done here is create the environment, to allow the law of attraction to get you what you desire. Think about it now, being this person, *"You being the creator; you creating in your life, situations and circumstances which are in harmony with your dominant thoughts."*

Do you see why if your dominant thoughts are confident, relaxed, happy and grateful, that your life situations and circumstances are then in harmony with your dominant thoughts. This allows you to become a master at manifesting.

Do you now see why people struggle to get the law of attraction to work for them? They have not created the right environment, as they have to have it first, before they can have it. The law of attraction is a law and has to be done in the right way, to be used to create the outcome you desire.

You provide the feelings of having had something and the law of attraction will go to work for you. Do you see how by you applying this, then it will be easy for you to master the law of attraction? Or does your ego still think it's impossible for you...

Well, by now, I'd say you're feeling a lot more confident that you can actually become a real life master of the law of attraction and that I'm not promising something I can't deliver to you.

But let's remove all the doubt and make sure you can stop thinking it's impossible once and for all... Okay?

Chapter 7:

It's Impossible!

The only limit you have is your own imagination. You've probably heard that before, and probably ignored the power of it too, as the last thing your ego wants is you knowing this is true… Let alone living it as *a way of life*.

I'm going to share a few stories over the next couple of chapters including one impossible story about health and the limitless power we have to do the impossible. And in later chapters I'll show you some more impossible things happening too… As I share these stories, they may seem a bit fantastic, or impossible to achieve… They're not. They just look it.

The law of attraction is like any tool and, the better you get at using it, the more and more impossible work you can do. Over countless tiny manifestations like computers as a kid, and parking spaces as an adult, I gradually got better and better at using the law of attraction. You have an advantage over me, it took me years to realise what I was doing was happening because *I thought it would*.

I wasted years of not knowing this stuff was happening on purpose, knowing what I know now, I could've created so much more. But when I figured it out, I sat down and really dared to dream big. You may or may not wish to do that yet, as your ego will want to knock you down if you dream too big, before you can control it. Or you may just decide, *"Stuff it, I'm doing it."* Everything is your choice.

As you read the stories, I suggest you attempt to consider the mindset I had along the way. See what you think was going on in my mind to achieve the results and then see how you had the same mindset too about when you were succeeding at things. Don't be intimidated by size, as the scale is only there to inspire. Success on any level is achieved through the same mindset process, because it's a universal law and can be replicated.

Okay, first off, we need to deal with you seeing things as possible as opposed to impossible. Because whatever you think is possible or impossible will end up being your reality. So we have to make you seeing anything you want as possible without any *positive thinking*, and definitely without *hoping it'll happen* or relying on luck for it to happen.

Napoleon Hill said, *"Desire is the starting point of all achievement, not a hope, not a wish, but a keen pulsating desire which transcends everything."*

We are taught by the experts to dream big, that this is the answer. Well, yes, it is, but that's *what to think* again, not *how to think*. So here's how to dream big, but first

40

you need to understand what goes on when virtually all people attempt to dream up something big.

For this example, I'll use Richard Branson to make the point. But this can be anything you once dreamed, or rather started to dream big on. Let's say someone gets inspired by what Richard Branson has achieved.

They start to consider that they too can build a big business. They sit back and enjoy the feeling of what it would be like to do it. Then they start to consider how they would build it, how they would get there. They begin to fill in the blanks. They begin to consider how it could be possible in a good way.

But now their ego begins to throw things in like, *"This is too hard."* And *"You've never done this before."* Or *"You're not as clever as Richard Branson."* Small tiny and irrelevant doubts are thrown into the dream pot and mixed around.

Soon enough, the dream begins to be killed by these doubts and, instead, now it's time to *build something realistic instead*, like a small business maybe and only maybe... Because *"You don't want to risk what you've got."* And so the fear of failure card is played by the ego.

Now if the dream wasn't nearly dead already, then it is by now. The chance of the person being another Richard Branson, or doing something greater, is disappearing fast. And the likelihood of despondency and regret in life is moving in to yet another person who just dared to dream big for a few short seconds.

The experts of course will tell people how to handle the fear of failure with more *what to think* information. *"Feel the fear and do it anyway."* *"Everything you want is on the other side of fear."* These quotes, and thousands more just like them, are supposed to inspire a person through their fear of failure.

And they work for the 1 in 100 people who succeed. But those people would've found a way through anyway, without the inspiring quotes... The 1 in 100 didn't need their help. So all that beautiful *what to think* information isn't helping solve the problem for the 99 in 100. They need *how to think* information. They need something that helps solve the problem, not something that makes them feel bad for *not being able to feel the fear and do it anyway*.

The problem is that, because there is no structured thinking for someone dreaming big, then when they attempt it, the ego can easily prevent it and stop their progress... When manifesting, and you're at the creating part of the dream, you can only look at the how to get there if you are just daring to dream *without limitation*. You can only do this safely if you can silence your ego.

When I dream big, I sit there and just consider possible ways it could happen. Not that it will happen, just that it could.

For example, when I conceived my Bug Free Mind Structured Thinking Process after I found the missing piece in personal development work, I sat there and thought, *"How can I write the most effective work on personal development there's ever been…"* (I think it's fair to say, that was a big dream as there's a LOT of great work out there)… And I thought, *"Well if I want to have the life I've just designed for myself, then that's what I must do to achieve it."*

So I said to myself in a very matter of fact way, *"Let's get on with it then."* And I began to write. I expected to solve the problem along the way and, because I thought I would, I could, and did.

If I'd doubted I could because it was *"too hard"* or, *"I'd never done it before,"* and there were *"far more clever authors out there than me who hadn't just failed so spectacularly, so who the heck did I think I was,"* then I wouldn't have achieved it. But I didn't. I dreamed big and saw what my life would be like having achieved it. I saw the benefit to everyone else too and I sort of instantly became responsible for creating it, as many were searching and I knew I could help.

Then I just considered ways it could be possible in a very calm and relaxed way, without any judgement. I simply decided that if I wanted to *actually have happen in real life* the dream, I had just had happen in my mind, that I would simply need to write the most effective work ever on getting people results.

Now, because my ego was not allowed to throw rocks at me (because I am the controller of my thoughts), I was free to dare to dream big. And when my ego eventually managed to chuck the odd rock or two I saw them as *'not helping me to bring my reality into everyone else's,'* so the rocks it threw dissolved into nothing before they could damage my dream.

You cannot work on how, unless you are the controller of your thought, or else any big dreams you create, your ego will destroy with its doubts.

So the secret is to not look for the *how it must happen*, just *how it could happen*. Just come up with ideas and show your mind how it's possible, exactly how isn't your job, that's the work of your subconscious mind.

Your job is to show your subconscious mind what you desire. I showed mine my future life of success. I had just failed spectacularly and very publicly, now the future I wanted was total vindication by teaching people how they could succeed at anything.

Incidentally, I read in 2012 that Napoleon Hill, the author of probably the best known book on success, Think and Grow Rich, actually began writing his work on teaching success right after he failed too. This made me feel quite good.

I digress… So in the process of creating the dream, you just look at *how it could happen* and show your subconscious mind possible ways to get there. You keep filling your mind with data, until you reach the point where you feel it is real. No positive thinking, instead you feel that this is real and is without a doubt going to happen in your future… At this point, you can be excited and love it, as you'll have passed the barrier of knowing it's real and have uploaded your instruction 100%.

From there, you are now looking for ways to bring this into your, and everyone else's, physical reality, as to not do so would feel wrong. Your ego's attempts to destroy your big dream are seen as unhelpful, so you don't fight your ego, you see it as more of an uneducated annoyance and so, without effort, dismiss its attempts to keep you down.

Also, as I said before, keep your eyes open for strange coincidences. Because it is highly likely that you've manifested them and they are in fact not just odd coincidences. The more you notice these things, the more and more confidence you attain in your ability to create your dreams.

Your work is learning how to ask for something in the right way, so that your subconscious mind gets it. This is where you focus your energy in manifesting. Remember your subconscious mind does not think in words, it thinks in feelings and in pictures. You show it yourself in the future and you show it possible ways to get there in feelings and pictures and it will find the exact route how for you.

For example, one of the routes to getting my Bug Free Mind work well know was, or is, doing a PR book tour in America. I knew a lot of best selling authors as friends and a lot of them had done the TV and radio talk show tour in the States, so I saw this as one potential way.

In early 2012, I began working again with an old business partner of mine, when I asked him to come and work with me at changing the world with my Bug Free Mind work. We sat and discussed the next few years and, at the time, I said to him that, early next year (2013), we would probably need to find an expert to help us do a talk show tour of the states.

That's all I said, I put no more effort in than that. But previously, I had considered this a potential route for me to take and saw how it was one of many possible routes.

Early January 2013, I'm in Miami, Florida, and about to go on a Caribbean cruise. At a networking event before the cruise, I meet two people who were experts at helping authors get on these tours. Then, while on the cruise, another expert on exactly the same thing approaches me. Then, over the next two months, three more different people, all in exactly the same field, approach us.

By this time, I had decided that I didn't want to take this route but I still had more people coming to me. In the end, there were eight different contacts, all of whom were experts in that field that came to me. I didn't go to them. Now, I hadn't even noticed that these guys had come to me through manifesting. My friend Pete said, you brought all these people to us by saying you wanted this to happen.

I had since changed my mind but my subconscious had done its job and gone out to the universe, connected with all these different people and engineered coincidences that meant they contacted us. Right now, you're probably thinking, sure, I'm a mark to them. That's how they make their money, right?

Well, this manifestation isn't going to let you off that easy. Five out of these eight had read my Bug Free Mind Process and felt they had to help me share it with people. They came to us through the law of attraction. The other three I met on the cruise and they just liked us.

Pete said to me that these people wouldn't leave him alone and wanted to introduce me for free to people and I kept saying no. It got so bad that he said his time was being taken up by attempting to explain why I didn't want this to happen, so much, that could I stop manifesting it. So I consciously had to tell my subconscious mind to distract them. So Pete stopped getting the calls, now they just email him occasionally, asking if I'm ready yet.

Consider this for a second, I know I can ask to have anyone I want come into my life to help me. My uncle told me this would happen and I live to it. I just haven't wanted to see many people yet though, when I wanted to meet Steve Wozniak, the speed at which that happened was very cool.

When you stop your ego throwing rocks at your dreams by not allowing them to affect your dream, then you are free to dream big. You are free to consider how things could happen without the burden of your ego wanting you to prove how that route can be realistic. Instead, you are free to dream. So it is the removal of doubt which is the secret, it is not to think positively. I do not think positively, I just do not think negatively. Then all that remains is positive. This is far easier to achieve than to always think positively.

Do you see how the impossible is possible yet?

Well, I'm guessing right now you can see how it's possible for me and you probably know for a fact that you've found someone who can walk the talk. But you're probably still doubting your own ability, given the fact of all the previous examples that have happened in your life.

That's okay, we are still only part way through this. There's a lot more mindset shifts still to come and I want to show you some really impossible stuff too. But, for a second, consider this...

When you become a master of the law of attraction, you actually have to become wary of what you are creating with your dreams, as you create so easily that you can have anything... Consider for a second if you would like to, what a wonderful problem that would be to have...

Becoming aware

One thing you must do to master the law of attraction is to become aware. I'm going to share with you a few more stories and show you how you must learn to pay attention to what's being presented to you, yes it really can have been you that created it... Remember to consider my state of mind as we go through. Pause at any time to consider.

The first story is of when I created my perfect partner and brought her into my life. Before I start, I should say that we're not able to affect others with the law of attraction unless they are looking for what we want too.

The story happened in 1988, when I was 21 years old... I had recently split up with a girlfriend and I was considering finding the perfect person for me. Then I suddenly thought, *"So we're just supposed to bump into the person we are going to spend the rest of our lives with, are we? Who came up with this plan, this is a dumb plan."*

I sat there and realised that the world was following a dumb plan and that this was probably why there were so few happy people about. So I considered what other ways there were to find a person. This was years before internet dating sites, or the internet!

I realised that I didn't actually know what I wanted in a person. I had a vague wishy washy idea of a beautiful girl but nothing much more than that. So I picked up a piece of paper and proceeded to design my perfect partner.

I decided she had to live within a radius of 10 miles of me and that she had to live or work within 100 yards of where I travelled. I put together every detail of what she looked like. I listed out exactly what she liked to do in life and how I was going to be the perfect centre of attention for her. I looked at our future together and saw how I never wanted her thinking of divorce, so her parents needed to be happily married so that she expected that outcome for herself too. I wanted her to have an older brother or sister. I even designed that her parents would want to babysit for us. I also designed the fact that she'd love me too, including all my faults.

I went on and on designing my perfect partner. I added in every tiny detail I could think about. While I was doing this, I began to see this girl in my mind and I had this feeling that she was real and that she, in fact, was looking for me too. I felt that when she saw me, she would fall in love with me instantly. This girl felt so real to me, that I felt I should give her a name. It didn't need to be her name, just my favourite girl's name which, of course, was Alison, as my favourite cousin was Alison. Now she felt so real, that I felt she was looking for me, too.

After a few hours and feeling pretty wonderful, I stopped designing her. What I didn't know at the time, as this was the first time I'd really done it, was that I had uploaded my design 100%. It was done, I had placed my order to the universe and shown my subconscious mind exactly what it had to go and get for me. So I just went about my day, knowing that I would be finding the person soon.

The next morning, I drove to work and noticed in a shop I drove past, a very pretty girl. This was the first girl I'd seen since designing my perfect partner. I thought, *"She's pretty. I'll have to stop there some time."*

Then I thought, *"I wonder if she's the one?"* To which my ego quickly replied, *"Don't be daft, you only designed this yesterday."* So I doubted it and went on with my life. A couple of weeks later, I slowed down enough to remember to go into the shop. By now I'd found a couple of potential perfect partners. But when I saw her, I had the feeling *I was supposed to know her.*

Sure enough, after considering her for a while, I decided it was her and that I needed to sweep her off her feet. Now I was the eldest of two brothers, talking to girls did not come easily to me. So I needed to find a way where actions could speak, or I'd fumble my words, as I instinctively knew I wanted it too much. The relationship, not sex, though that definitely came up too. So, whilst driving to work, I considered how a chance meeting could occur…

On the following Sunday, I was playing cards with my brother and he asked me how it was going on the girlfriend front. I said I'd found one I really liked and was just figuring out the best way to approach her. He asked me where she came from and I told him she worked in a newsagent in Storrington. *"Not the one as you go into Storrington?"* he said…

"Yes." He asked me if she had long brown hair. I said yes. *"Her name's not Alison is it?"* he asked… No, at the time, I had forgotten I had designed her name to be Alison, I only realised I'd done that when I found my design years later…

I said, *"Yes, that's her name,"* at which point my brother just said, *"Oh no. I don't believe it. How can this happen?"* It turned out that he had already asked her out and she'd turned him down. Fortunately at the time, I was blessed with good looks, something that time has taken from me in the cruelest of ways possible. But then, I was good looking.

It turned out that this was the girl who'd given him a dodgy phone number to get rid of him and then, not being put off, my brother had spent a day and a half driving round Storrington to find where she lived. I said to him, *"You know where she lives! Give me her address."*

I knew she was going to be perfect for me and so did my brother, he saw right then that his elder brother was going to be spending a lot of time with the girl who had not wanted to go out with him... He emigrated to Tasmania a few years later, I'm not saying it bothered him but this was as far away as he could go... Only joking!

So I drove round to her home the following Friday night, as I knew she fancied me and stalking is allowed when you're young. I knocked on the door, spoke to her mum and then she came to the door and I could see she was blown away.

We've been together ever since; life just continues to get better with her. I love all the time we get to spend together and the sex is great too!

Fortunately, my subconscious mind showed her to me more than once, it was actually several times before I actually stopped. But if I hadn't become aware, then I may have missed her.

The problem was I allowed my ego to convince me to doubt that finding her (*the one person in the world for me*), could've happened in less than 24 hours and, in fact, be the very first girl I saw after designing her... I doubted it...

But think about it...why not? I'd created a near perfect design, she was perfect for me and I was perfect for her, because I put me into the design for her, too. In fact, the only fault she has is that she doesn't like, in fact, she hates, personal development books. She thinks I'm a bit weird for writing them and she thinks you're weird for reading them.

When I invite her to come and meet people when I teach occasionally, she says, "I don't want to meet weirdos who are into that stuff." Then, when she meets them, she says they're really nice. Funny that, people who are into self-improvement being nice people. The problem is that I didn't know personal development books existed when I designed her, so I didn't put that into her design.

One reason I think it happened so fast was that she was looking for me too and there was nothing left to be done. This was a near perfect manifestation. The funny thing was that, after designing her, I never looked at the design again. I didn't do anything the experts tell you to do with goals where it comes to looking at the goal daily.

I had uploaded my design 100% and now it was time to work diligently on bringing my design into everyone else's reality… Especially hers! I really never looked at the design again. In fact it was only in 2005 or 2006, when I was listening to a Tony Robbins' CD, where he said you should design your perfect partner, that I remembered I'd even done it nearly two decades before.

I went home and told Alison the whole story, as I'd never explained it before, to which she said how unromantic it was and wasn't happy with the fact that she was my goal. Until this year, she saw it as unromantic and then was working next to me (we work together at home, she runs our investments and I write and build the business). She was there and I was checking the video footage from a Life Design Getaway seminar I'd just done. I don't do many seminars but, in 2014, I taught the design process I used to create her and travelled round the world for six weeks teaching it. Actually that six-week world tour being paid to speak was another thing I manifested, too.

In 2010, I sat down and figured out all the things I wanted to do and one was travel around the world being paid to speak and travel with my friend, Pete. But I was open to an even greater manifestation and, in 2014, I got to tour the world, being paid to speak and travel with two friends, Pete and Tim. I digress again…

One of the ideas behind the world tour was that, by the time I got back to England, I'd be good enough to be filmed and I could turn the content into a short video course, rather than doing these one day seminars again. I did this live, because the design process is not something that translates well to written or audio. It needs to be taught live, as we do a lot of direct communication with your subconscious mind and that can be almost impossible without body language to help get the message across. The live recording of the design process is available for purchase online.

Anyway, at times, she was listening and watching the footage of the seminar, as she's still never seen me speak. I obviously told the story of designing her, my perfect partner. I didn't think she was listening but, after it had finished, she said, *"I'm glad I didn't come and see you, as I would've burst into tears."* She had finally seen it in the romantic way it was meant.

So, is less than 24 hours impossible? Obviously not! Improbable certainly, but not impossible… So don't doubt your ability to do the impossible a, in doing so, you are killing the possibility of it…

But why not? She wanted me, so why couldn't it happen within 24 hours? Now, making millions took a little longer and, depending on how you are going to do it, can take a while, or a long while. As long as you don't doubt the impossible, you have a good chance. All you are doing is allowing the improbable the possibility of happening. After all, if you drop a coin on the ground enough times, eventually it'll end up on its side. But it is highly improbable…

Your job as a master of the law of attraction is to just *not get in the way of it happening*. You have to work diligently on providing a set of circumstances that enable the improbable to have more of a chance and the easiest way to do this is to first *get out of your own way by not doubting it.*

Now, if you think using the law of attraction to find a perfect partner who has your favourite girl's name is impossible… then how about this…

When I Was Crippled

All areas of life can be resolved using the law of attraction IF you think they can…

Back in 2003, I was crippled with a disc in my back being twisted slightly and putting pressure on my sciatic nerve. It felt like someone had stuck a dagger into the nerve at the centre of my leg and they were wiggling it about. This pain would start in my leg and just destroy my ability to do anything and I spent months in agony. The problem was I *needed* to be fixed, so that I was not either crippled or in agony for the rest of my life.

I decided to 'try' everything. However, I knew this would be fixed. I never doubted that, as I saw me living my life without the pain, though the only caveat I had was to not have an operation. I did not 'want' my spine hacked about with.

I had suffered with a bad back for years and was used to spending 5 to 10 days a year crippled. Up until this point, I had considered that an acceptable trade for the damage I had undoubtedly done to my back, through years of abuse on site. Though I did dream about never having a bad back again, whilst my ego did what it could to tell me how that was impossible.

But, thanks to the excruciating sciatic pain, I decided that I had had enough of all of this and I 'wanted' rid of bad back pain and sciatic pain for good. I reached an absolute decision; I would be rid of this pain for good! It wasn't a request, it was an instruction. I also dreamed about how wonderful my life would be when I was no longer in this pain and that was what I had to bring into my reality.

So my goal was my back being fixed permanently and no operation in the process. Totally unrealistic I know, but I also knew this would happen, as it felt right. I then set out to 'try' absolutely every possible cure (providing multiple solutions). I was working diligently on creating the probability of a cure. I would 'try' different practitioners as well and multiple sessions (I would not assume that because one person was an expert in, say, acupuncture, that they were all the same). You name it, I 'tried' it and I 'tried' it more than once.

But, after a couple of months, I was losing the will to live. I had 'tried' stacks and nothing had made *even the slightest difference*. You know the feeling you get when something feels different (a little better) and you know it? Well, I didn't have even the smallest feeling of that after every conceivable treatment.

I felt totally trapped so, in the end, I relented and went to see the doctor, I knew what they'd say... *"You need an operation."* She had best intentions of course and told me how she'd have me fixed in no time with an operation. There was nothing to worry about, as her husband had had the same thing, a quick op and it was all fixed. The next day, I went and saw a specialist, had an MRI scan done and he said almost the same thing.

Everything in my body said, *"yes, this would fix it now but would not fix it forever!"* I also knew that, once this was done, it couldn't be undone and I knew I was at a crossroads which would either free me from pain for good, or end up with a quick fix now and then pain for the rest of my life, which would begin at some point in the future. This wasn't the solution I was looking for.

Don't get me wrong, this was not an expert's opinion, these were my instincts about what was logical. At the crossroads where the route *'freedom from pain for good'* was marked, the road looked like it had no end in sight. No promise of hope and no idea where it would lead. This was definitely the long painful route. The other direction had a warm hospital with friendly people offering an immediate fix.

I relented and agreed to the operation. It was booked for 3 weeks time. Although, despite the constant pain and the fact that I hadn't slept on a bed for months or had more than an hour's sleep without waking in pain, I decided that I would continue to seek an alternative solution right up until the operation.

A couple of weekends before the operation I was at a wedding and had to have a chair with me all of the time. I was dosed up on my usual 30+ painkillers a day. I, of course, mixed that with as much alcohol as I could, as the pain was bad.

Then a friend I hadn't seen for several years said he was doing some work for a guy who was having him do some plumbing in his new restaurant. He told me this guy reckoned he could cure any bad back with a wooden stick. By this time, I had actually given up and paid lip service to my friend's suggestion.

I said I would call the guy with the wooden stick on Monday but had no intention of doing so. After all, this guy was a chef, not a back specialist. Then on my way back from my hotel room at the wedding, I bumped into my friend again in a corridor and he happened to be on the phone to the chef.

I was drunk by this time and still in agony but he put me on the phone and I thought *why not* - I said I'd call him Monday to set up an appointment. I called him and set up a time for Wednesday. I was in such a bad way that I had to ask my friend Pete (yes, the same Pete) to drive me, as I could no longer drive. I had stacks of Ferraris and Lamborghinis but could no longer drive… That was surreal in itself!

Now everything about this was wrong; he was a chef not a bad back specialist, he didn't have a treatment table, he had a coffee table. He didn't have a surgery; he had a one bedroom flat with a front room. He didn't have a certificate on his mantelpiece, he had models of Chinese weapons. He didn't have a receptionist; he had a mate watching children's TV in the middle of the day.

This was all so very, very wrong! Yet somehow, I knew he would fix it. His professional diagnosis only took about 30 seconds with me standing there in front of him in his front room with his mate watching children's TV and me now dressed only in my boxer shorts. And oh, did I mention that Brighton is the gay capital of the UK and where he lived was the height of the gay district? Also, I had zero ability to fend off any unwanted advances! Talk about hitting a low point!

Anyway, his highly professional 30 second diagnosis which was said in a strong Chinese accent was, *"Owwwar, your back it fu**ed!"* which inspired my confidence no end! Nevertheless, he told me he could only cure it 99% and it would take weekly treatments over 18 months. I was not really paying that much attention to the 18 months but I had heard the 99% fixed very clearly and I heard the truth in what he was saying… This wasn't just some chef who could massage backs, too. I knew this guy was something special.

I had a treatment, which was not pain-free. In fact, it was excruciatingly painful and I screamed so much that even his friend got off the sofa and went and watched children's TV in the bedroom! My torturer said to me that I had to give up all painkillers, to which I told him they were keeping me alive.

He told me to come back next Wednesday for another treatment. I had zero intention of ever letting him anywhere near my back again! But when I got off of the coffee table and stood up, *something* was different. As Bill Murray said in Groundhog Day, *"Anything different is good."* I walked outside and the pain was… well… less.

I went home and cancelled the operation. The following week I went back for a treatment and was down to one painkiller a day, the following week I was down to none and have never taken a painkiller since for anything other than a hangover.

Within a few weeks, I was back up to 80% fixed and 18 months later to the week, I was fixed! The rest is history; I don't have a bad back anymore. He cured that, just as he said he would. He also removed 99% of the arthritis I had in my hands from the years on the tools. I also never had the back operation and he became a good friend. He gave me my first real wellness experience and he changed my life. I no longer suffer with a bad back... ever!

However, if I do something to make me have a bad back, like sitting typing non-stop for three weeks, I know whatever damage I've done can be undone simply.

So what the heck happened? This guy wasn't a back specialist before I met him - I mean, he was but he was a chef and wasn't practising his treatments. After my first book on making money, I told this same story and then he gave up being a chef because he treated so many of my book buyers and cured all sorts of ailments for them.

But just imagine the power of my goal-setting to manifest what I did. I knew it would work; in fact, the only point I actually gave up knowing it was during the conversation with my friend who was telling me about him... I almost missed becoming aware... But my subconscious mind was there to help me with bumping into my friend in the corridor when he was on the phone to him... Impossible, right?

So what happened? Simple; I had created this. He was the only person doing this treatment in the UK and I had never heard about it before and when I Googled it, neither had they! There were zero results on Google!

Until April 2014, I had never heard of anyone else in the world doing it, then when I was on the world tour, teaching the life design technique, I told this story and a lady told me that she's had the treatment done by a man in Egypt and how it had fixed her too. And how she'd asked for a cure and found him but, until I told my story, she hadn't realised she'd manifested the same cure too.

But, apart from the guy in Egypt, as far as I have been able to find out, he is the only person in the world doing it!

I asked him once how old the treatment was and he said he didn't know. He had been crippled himself and was carried by his friends to an old Chinese guy, who took 18 months to fix him. He had then asked this Chinese guy to teach him and in return he would sweep up and work for the old guy. This was a dying Chinese art and I had uncovered it to solve my bad back and sciatic pain.

Just think about how improbable all of this is... I tried every alternative therapy you could name, and some you couldn't. I tried multiple therapists to make sure I hadn't picked one that was no good... Finally I gave in and tried conventional medicine! I was certain there was another way but the pain was simply impossible to bear.

Then this guy lived within 20 miles of me and he wasn't in the business; he was a chef and had moved to the UK a few years before and had never treated ANYONE in the UK... I was the first one. Most people didn't have to endure the pain I did, as he was very rusty when he first worked on me.

What are the odds against this? Think about what life giving power I had just discovered, I could cure the incurable just by knowing I could. This taught me the power of manifestation.

I made a decision and I knew that, despite what every expert said, I would make it happen. My back was fixed for good, with no operation. How cool is that?

So, is it impossible to find a cure when it's not possible? The answer is... It depends on one thing... If you think you can find the impossible, then it's possible. If you think you cannot find it, then it really is impossible. You can shape your health with your mind. I live this as *a way of life*.

I have since cured all things as they come up and this wellness experience inspired me to learn more and more about health. I could write at least one book on what I discovered and have cured in myself and in others.

But we already know we can fix things with just our minds... Doctors have known this for centuries... A doctor will often give their patient a placebo medication, as they know that if they think they are being given a cure then they will just get better... So why do we always think we need medication when we already know that our minds are capable of curing us at least some of the time? And, in my experience, all of the time... Well, we only know it on an intellectual level; we don't know it on *a way of life*, level. So we don't know it, do we?

Some more proof that this impossible stuff is true comes from the wonderful Dr Émile Coué.

Émile Coué was a French psychologist and pharmacist who introduced a popular method of psychotherapy and self-improvement based on *optimistic auto-suggestion*.

The application of his mantra-like conscious auto-suggestion, *"Every day, in every way, I'm getting better and better."* Or *"Day by day, in every way, I'm getting better and better."* The Coué method centred on a routine repetition of this particular expression according to a specified ritual - preferably as much as twenty times a day and especially at the beginning and at the end of each day.

Coué maintained that curing some of our troubles requires a change in our unconscious thought, which can be achieved only by using our imagination. Although stressing that he was not primarily a healer but one who taught others to heal themselves, Coué effected organic changes through auto-suggestion.

Coué observed that the main obstacle to auto-suggestion was willpower. For the method to work, the patient must refrain from making any independent judgement, meaning that he must not let his will impose its own views on positive ideas. Everything must thus be done to ensure that the positive *'auto-suggestive'* idea is consciously accepted by the patient; otherwise the patient may end up getting the opposite effect of what is desired.

For example, when a student has forgotten an answer to a question in an exam, he will likely think something such as, *"I have forgotten the answer"*. The more he or she tries to think of it, the more the answer becomes blurred and obscured. However, if this negative thought is replaced with a more positive one, *"No need to worry, it will come back to me,"* the chances that the student will come to remember the answer will increase.

Coué was given the opportunity to work with countless terminally-ill patients, who were often sent to him when they were expected to live for only a couple more weeks. What happened next was impossible and is still considered impossible. But something in the region of 90% of the terminally-ill patients *just didn't die*. They got better and they left.

Coué had come up with a way to fix all kinds of diseases, even terminally-ill ones, using the law of attraction... So just imagine for a second you were me and you were living a way of life where you knew you could fix anything that came up. How relaxed and comfortable would you be? You can master the law of attraction to do the impossible for you too... IF you don't doubt it and just think you can.

Your immune system will heal itself. Parts of our bodies are replaced every day, every week, every month, every year... Within a few years we have a brand new body. So all you have to do is not get in your own way by doubting it.

My mum believed in her doctor so much that, last year, it nearly killed her. I offered to help her with the real cure, as I knew the medication was her problem. But she knew the medication was her cure.

She steadily got worse and worse. Alison said to me, can't I help her and I said, *"She has to be ready, she's got to be desperate enough for me to help her."* One day, she showed up at our home and I actually saw that she had less than a year to live. She looked very ill and was depressed and broken.

I asked her, *"are you ready to be cured of this yet, Mum?"* to which she replied, *"Of course I am!"* I told her that it would mean questioning what she knew was true. She said she'd do anything, as she'd lost 42 lbs in 3 months and was sick daily and had near constant diarrhoea.

So I told her to get her medicine, I went on Google and typed name of medicine + "side effects". The first article came up from the National Health Service. The first line said, if you are suffering from sickness or diarrhoea, then stop taking this immediately.

I turned to my mum and said, *"Can't your doctor use Google? Or maybe he can't type a question in."* Instantly, I broke the bond my mum had with her doctor and she saw how she could be healed…

I think it was 5 or 6 of her medications that all said stop taking immediately if you had those symptoms. The other 3 or 4 were all giving her something that she lacked in her diet. So I designed a new diet for her and showed her how the minerals she needed that were in the medications, she could get from food.

We halved her remaining medication to wean her off of them slowly and she began her new lifestyle. Two days later, she was well enough to see friends again. Two weeks later, she was well and has remained so. I told her not to tell her doctor but she did and he was so grateful she was well, as he had been trying everything he could to help her…

But the key point which I haven't shared with my mum is that she now thinks she can control her health. She now thinks she can fix herself, so she does. Occasionally, she shows up and says she's ill again and I ask her what medication he's put her back on… She tells me and I go online and show her that it's the medication causing her side effects, or how to remove them with food. It can be tricky to make new tricks stick when teaching an old… I'll leave that analogy alone.

As we age, it becomes harder and harder to alter the neurons in our minds, because they are deeply engrained. So sometimes we will revert back to the old ways, even after we have proved to our self that the new way works and the old way doesn't… So an awareness of that will help, if you can make it part of your life. If you cannot, then it will probably be destructive.

W. Clement Stone said, *"Whatever the mind of man can conceive, it can achieve."* My mum can now conceive health. I can now conceive that I can create the impossible. You are only limited by what you can conceive.

I like to set a goal so big that if I achieve it, it will blow my mind. But each time I do that, I see how it's actually likely to happen now I've considered it as a possibility. Then you get into the world of thinking, *"If I can have anything, then exactly what do I want? I must be careful!"*

How do you feel about achieving the impossible now? Remember, I am showing you big manifestations to demonstrate what's possible, do not let the scale intimidate, as the process for manifesting big and small is the same.

Before leaving this, I would like to tell you if you'll let me, what BIG goal I set for myself and how I'm doing at creating it now... Bear in mind I gave myself at least 20 hours thought regarding this goal, but then it's pretty big and audacious...

Chapter 8:

You Can Have Anything You Think You Can!

In January, 2010, I was in the first few weeks of creating my new life and fortune. I had fulfilled my duty to my trustees and now it was time to make money again, as that's just what I'd always done, so I was about to do it again.

I came up with a simple business strategy to get rich again. I saw a trend in a certain business model and saw how I could position myself as the expert in it and make a lot of money whilst helping other businesses along the way. I spent about two weeks working on it and decided who I'd pitch it to first and use that business as the foundation to creating another success in my life.

All the time I was creating the model and the pitch, I knew it was going to work. But I was still a little uncomfortable, as there were areas I didn't really want to have in my life. But my training kicked in and said, *"No, don't be such a wimp, you'll just deal with them as you always do."*

So I carried on and pitched it. I was going to take a local business from £800k turnover to £2,300k. I'd do it in one to two years and it would turn their net profit from less than £20k to circa £400k. I also guaranteed to save the company more than I would ask them for as a fee. Plus, they could pay me over time and, if what I did didn't work, then they could keep all the work I'd done, not pay me any commission and I'd also return the fee.

Now if you're not in business then you may not know, but that's what's known as an irresistible offer. Which is why I knew the owner would rip my arm off. But he didn't. He said no... I was stunned... How could this not work?

As I drove home, I realised why it hadn't worked. Because everything always works out for the best for me and the very last thing I actually wanted to do was go once again into a business I didn't love and just do a business because I could, not because I should.

By the time I got home, I was over the moon, I was so grateful for the bullet I just dodged. As I walked through the door, Alison said, *"He bought, then?" "No, isn't it wonderful! I nearly made the same mistake again but, thankfully, he said no!" "What are you going to do now to make money then?" "I'm going to sit on the sofa for a few months and think about what I want to do with the rest of my life."* Obviously Alison was not that impressed but she came round later.

So I sat down and spent time thinking about what I loved to do and eventually, after a lot of thought, I found a mission that was worthy of my life. While this was going on, I still had a small community site with a few hundred members on it and they were still asking me to write on how to make money.

I thought that would be absolutely ridiculous. I'd just lost tens of millions; the last thing I wanted to do was profess to be this guy who could teach people how to make money. Maybe in the future, when I had made another fortune I thought, but not now. So I told everyone that and as people had been asking me how my mindset could be so strong at such a bad time, I said I'd write about how to achieve that.

So I started writing and people loved it, I was solving some real issues for them like depression, worry, fear. And I was enjoying writing it, too. When I wasn't writing, I was thinking, or learning new skills. It was a very enjoyable time in my life.

So, in one of my many times of thinking, I worked out that *the world had a maths problem.* The problem was there were too few successful people breeding too few successful children and there were too many unsuccessful people breeding too many unsuccessful children. I saw that, one day, the world would likely be overwhelmed by unsuccessful people.

A couple of years later, in 2012, I saw the film *Idiocracy,* which is a satirical science fiction comedy film about exactly that happening.

I saw that depression, frustration, anger, despair and all the other nasties, would grow and eventually things wouldn't get better for my children's descendants; life would actually be worse. I remember my dad saying to me once, that his childhood was better than mine and, in turn, I saw how mine was better than my children's. So I thought something needs to change; what could I do?

I mixed that around in my head with all the thoughts I'd discovered about why I could succeed and I was still considering why success books got such a low success rate.

Then I just saw it. All the pain and suffering was caused because people didn't know *how to think* as, once you know that, you stop causing yourself and others pain. Once that has happened, it actually becomes almost impossible to cause pain. So, if you can't cause others pain, then the ripple effect is that in the absence of pain, good is created without effort.

Simplified, the world sees the need, I saw the cause. If you remove the cause, then you automatically remove the need. There is a powerful saying which is something like, *the end of war will come only when people stop wanting to go to war.* This is obviously a long way off and will probably not happen in my lifetime but, if I taught people *how to think,* then they will always seek to avoid pain and gather much more pleasure in their life.

I concluded if I teach the masses, then my descendants will be okay, too. So I'd found my purpose, my mission. I would teach the world simple structured thinking and change the world, one mind at a time.

I then looked at what was needed to change the world, as there's a lot of people. Was there a tipping point which was an easier target for me? I researched it and found out that around 3.14% of the population needs to adopt something for it to be adopted by the majority. This meant I needed to get around 225 - 250 million people to go through the Bug Free Mind Process and they would do the rest for me. *Can you see me daring to dream?*

Now I'd found something worthy for me to do for the rest of my life! I had found a dream that was worthy of my ability. I sat there and dared to dream what was possible. The first thing I thought was, can I get to 250 million people? So I looked for an example. In 1937, Napoleon Hill wrote Think and Grow Rich and the book sells more today than it ever has. He's now sold somewhere between 70 and 150 million copies of his work.

Okay, I thought, *"this could take a while!"* So I looked for an easier example. Jack Canfield and Mark Victor Hansen had sold over 250 million copies of their Chicken Soup for the Soul books, so I studied how he achieved it and he used the law of attraction in a brilliant way.

Then my normal mindset came into play. I don't doubt my ability, *if someone else can do it then so can I*. So I used Jack and Mark's inspired work to inspire me and I decided to get on with it.

So I continued to dream and looked for ways to take it out of the personal development space and into the mainstream. I looked for ways to reach a wider market than the work was usually aimed at. So I conceived other markets and other ways to help people all based around the Bug Free Mind Process. I even saw how the process would one day end up in the school system but I thought that would happen maybe in twenty years.

As I was seeing this all play out while I was 'just looking', I could see that this idea would compensate me as well as help millions, and maybe even billions, of people along the way. I can tell you this dream felt really good! As I dreamt it, so it began to feel real and feel like I should do it. Not that I could but that I should. It felt like a compulsion.

So I sat back and decided to spend the rest of my life creating this wonderful dream and bring it into everyone else's reality. But there was a caveat, I would only do what I wanted to do. I would only create success on my terms and I wouldn't move on from one thing before I'd finished the bit I was working on. I was no longer prepared to rush, or be busy.

I wanted to enjoy every moment and not miss out on the journey. I wanted the journey to be my reward; the destination, if it was meant to happen within my lifetime, would come along at the right time and in the right way, as everything going forward was going to work out for the best for me. I was going to create massive success again but I was going to live to my core truth, *success on my terms!*

Thanks to the wonderful Napoleon Hill example, I saw how my work will continue to grow after I've gone. And I saw how he hadn't designed his work to do that, so I altered the design of mine before I begun to write.

It's 4 years and 8 months since I conceived my future plan. We haven't actually begun doing real business yet and we have achieved some extraordinary and nearly impossible to believe results.

Firstly, I completed the process and it is widely accepted by my peers in the field of personal development as the most effective work ever created. The people who use it know it is. Many of them are living it as *a way of life* and manifesting stuff, which blows me away.

I have people email me thanks from all over the world, daily. We currently ship to 129 countries and the process is still only in English. If I told you who I've turned down chatting with, you wouldn't believe me! I turned them down because the resulting chat would've taken me in directions I did not want to go in. But most people would've viewed that direction as success… But success on my terms, remember!

I've written the draft of a novel version of the process. I've written a draft movie trilogy. I've written a draft for a comedy series that crosses all borders, all cultures and all age groups. And currently, we are looking at potentially putting the A Bug Free Mind Process into one country's entire education system.

Actually, I said I'd tell that story; here's how I manifested something that is so bi, it's unreal!

I was abroad in a taxi with a friend a few years ago and said, *"I think I could teach this country."* Being similar to me, he didn't do what most people would do and attempt to kill the dream with helpful statements like, *"What, are you serious? You're mad, you'll never do that. After all, you're not an expert in normal education. They don't even know who you are."*

Perhaps someone has shot your dreams down in a similar way? No instead he just said, *"Do you think so?"* And I said, *"Yes!"* I left it there but continued to think of possible ways it could happen. Nothing more!

A few months later, I was teaching an event and a lady there said she knew 79 of the top 100 most influential people in that area of the world. This was opportunity presenting itself and I noticed it. Quick as a flash, I said, *"If I had your connections, I'd be changing the world."*

She was a successful businesswoman who was on the verge of another successful product launch. So I thought the timing wasn't right but maybe, in 3 to 5 years, we may be able to do something.

I continued to think about it while we were on the course and I recognised my own limitations. So I asked my friend Tim to work with me and see if he could pull anything together with this lady and me. His persistence was needed, as I wouldn't do what was required to bring it any further into reality. I wouldn't do it, because I thought it was too soon and I hadn't created enough proof yet. Plus she was busy elsewhere.

Anyway, Tim saw the possibility as he'd done the full Bug Free Mind Process, knew his own ability and had seen some magic happen a few times before, so why not this...

Behind the scenes, Tim worked with her to put me in a room with some of these influential people much earlier than we thought was possible. In fact, it was under a year. I was asked if I would create an extra days training course to teach the basics of the Bug Free Mind Process... Now I'm quite a lazy person, so I didn't really want to do this but did it anyway and ended up creating the presentation partly in the airport before we got there.

I was not told who the people were; well, I was, but I didn't understand their influence or, rather, I didn't bother to read the email properly. On the day I was told they would not participate, that they would just listen. I was also told they would leave after the first few hours. And I was told to curb some of my more descriptive lessons too. So I couldn't have fun and I had to be on my best behaviour!

Within the first few hours, the first person was in tears and could see what this would do for their country. By lunchtime, we were unofficially asked if we would be interested in putting it into some element of their education system. By now, everyone was joining in. By the end of the day, we had had a wonderful time and everyone loved what they'd seen. They came back the next day for the original presentation and we were officially asked to submit a proposal. At the end of the day, I was told who everyone was; a member of royalty, a member of parliament, advisors to the minister for education ...

The following day, we were invited to meet another member of royalty in their home. While presenting, I'd been explaining how I got my children to get A grades the easy way, without revising. So I was asked if I could help their daughter, as she had a biology exam the following week and was expecting a D grade. I chatted with her for about 20 minutes. Two weeks later, we heard her result, she had gone from D to A with just a 20-minute chat... *Magic, right?*

Since submitting our proposal, we were asked to write a vision for what I saw the outcome would be for the country if we put the system into their entire education system. Frankly, I felt honoured to be asked to write it. Right now, we are still working with them on how this can best work, so this manifestation is only part created and, if I didn't know that whatever happens will work out for the best for me, then I couldn't share it with you. But because I do, I can... no matter what that is.

In the meantime, four other countries have heard about it and approached us about talking to them.

Now, my effort in all of this has been nothing but tiny. I saw it as a possibility; I saw it as a wonderful way to get to my 250 million people figure within my lifetime. As let alone all the countries I can help, when the world sees the result, then there will be *a perception shift* in their understanding of just how the Bug Free Mind Process really can help them.

But none of this is about chasing money; I expect to get paid a fortune far, far bigger than anything I created before. But I am not in a rush, I am not chasing it, I do not need it, I am detached from it happening. Sure, it's happened in my mind and I'm working on bringing it into your and everyone else's reality. To achieve this, I am just doing the tiny bits I need to do when they are presented to me.

Just as my Uncle Dave told me, I have some bits missing, *don't worry, the people who have those bits will come to me and help.*

I thought this education idea would take about 20 years and, who knows, it may still do but, as I'm open and living my life to always being open to a greater manifestation then, who knows, maybe it'll happen sooner.

You are not here to try to get the world to be just as you want it. You are here to create the world around you that you choose. That's what I am living as *a way of life*. Can you see why it's easy for me to be a master of the law of attraction?

As I said at the start of this section... the only limit you have is your own imagination. I've shared with you some impossible stories and an impossible story that's still in progress. To use the law of attraction to your maximum potential, all you have to do is not limit your imagination and *choose to not doubt you can achieve the impossible*.

Consider if you will, do you see things as possible yet? Because seeing it as impossible will result only in it being impossible... So what benefits you?

"Desire is the starting point of all achievement, not a hope, not a wish, but a keen pulsating desire which transcends everything." My desire transcended the impossible and that was just a choice I made.

Buddha said, *"What you are is what you have been. Who you will be is what you do now."* Choice again, but now you can see the level at which you need to be aware of how you live your way of life, as that makes or breaks you when it comes to mastering the law of attraction...

Wallace D Wattles said, *"You are to become a creator, not a competitor; you are going to get what you want but in such a way that, when you get it, every other man will have more than he has now."* Can you see how I am living as a creator, not as a competitor? I am going to get what I want but, in such a way that, when I get it, every other person will have more than they have now...

This isn't just talking about living an abundant life. It is living abundance as *a way of life*. For you to become the master you are actually designed to be, you must today begin living every moment as a creator. Consider that for a while, if you want to...

Now look around you at the things you don't like in your life and ask yourself... *"What is it in me that is causing this situation to persist? What am I failing to learn, that is making life give me the same lesson again?"* If you can learn that then you can break out of any rut.

Why not consider that you are the architect of your life and you can change and improve it as you go along... *So what do you want to improve today?*

Then ask yourself the question above... This is living your life to the line, *if you change the way you look at things, then the things you look at will change*. This is a really simple thought structure that will improve the quality of your life from the moment you begin using it.

Now this goal of mine here may sound big, audacious and unrealistic but I finally found a mission that was worthy of me. I spent a lifetime playing it small, when those around me thought I was playing it big. This is living my life to the line, *'aim for the stars and you'll hit the sky.'*

But this is also living my life on my terms, doing what I want to do. Who knows what I'll achieve from it, maybe I'll go all the way, maybe I'll hit the tipping point, maybe I'll go further, who knows. What matters is I'm okay with whatever happens, as I'm enjoying the journey.

There is no disappointment, no fear of failure, no missing out, as I could be doing something better, something more worthy. I sat down and figured out what I wanted to do with the rest of my life and am currently doing it.

When you live your life knowing that deciding to walk in just one direction will eventually have a far greater result than constantly changing directions, then you can really start to make a difference.

One last thing, before finishing here…

I was in Las Vegas whilst on the world tour and one of my students who had previously been on a five day seminar with me had come along to this one-day event on designing.

I organised a day for just masterminding and he asked me something which you may find interesting. *"Is all this stuff supposed to be happening with my mind?"* *"What stuff do you mean?"* *"Everyone's my bitch!"* Alan is a younger successful guy, as you may have already figured out.

"What do you mean, Alan?" *"I can control people; if I think of someone, then within a few seconds they are ringing me. If I want someone to go out with me to a specific place, they call me and suggest that place. I seem to be able to control those around me and get them to do what I want? Is this supposed to be happening?"*

I answered him with, *"Yes, as long as you are doing things which will benefit others, then once you master your thinking you'll simply think the things you want and they will almost magically begin happening in this way."* Everyone there was a little surprised but I had the advantage of having with me someone who had experienced the intensive five-day training, so Alan made me look very good.

Just in case you're thinking you might like to go to a seminar one day, I don't do them anymore. I only did the seminars to learn how to be better at teaching my work and I got an amazing bounty when I did, which will take me years to get into print. Some of it's in this work here.

As Alan found, your thoughts are extremely powerful. They are like a form of mental energy that travels at the speed of light. They are so fine, they can go through any barrier. This is why, for example, you can think about a person, sometimes at a great distance and, in the next moment, the phone will ring and that person will be on the line. Your thoughts have connected with that person, the moment you thought of them.

You can take this further and not know the person too... As long as it is in their benefit to meet you, then you can manufacture some amazing coincidences.

Next, I'd like to share with you a couple of amazing stories from two of my students. All these guys have done is read the Bug Free Mind Process, though one of them came to the one day Life Design Getaway seminar I ran; as mentioned earlier, a recording of this is available for purchase online but I will not be doing any more live seminars.

I think you'll see after reading them, just what can be achieved when you master the law of attraction.

Chapter 9:

You Can Do It Too ...

I'm going to share with you two stories from guys who both happen to live in the UK and who've done at least one part of the Bug Free Mind Process.

The first guy, Seamus, has sent me regular feedback along the way, so I thought I'd share his journey with you here and you'll see how he began living the way and then it all nicely came together.

These came from Seamus McCrory – October 2012 to March 2014 – 18 months

1) Day 1 October 2012 - *I've just downloaded the free 5 chapter offer. I've just read the first two and feel compelled to leave feedback, Don't know why. Anyways, I've found myself smiling a lot and laughing out loud at the style and humour of your writing and observations. Hilarious! I love it. It's made me sit up and take notice, BIG style!*

I have "searched" for years on the personal development circuit, for ideas information and knowledge to break me through that barrier that's been holding me back for as long as I can remember. I'm all "guru--ed" as it were, until I've found this. I'm going to return to reading now and expect to purchase the full deal. Thanks for making me feel light-hearted

2) A few months in now - *Hey Andy, Thanks for email asking if I was enjoying the site. I am immensely, thank-you. I waded in and have immersed myself into the whole experience and my dominant attention is now nothing but ABFM reading, audio, video, YouTube, members' site. I've become friends with some people off the site and have skyped and texted.*

I read somewhere from you that the members site would act like a vacuum in my head for me, replacing negative thoughts with positive ones; jeepers, you were not kidding!! The site has acted like a rocket launcher!! Applying all I can as frequently as I can remember. Not watched TV for nearly 2 weeks, haven't read a newspaper for over 3 years, have affirmations stuck up all over the place. Feel I am becoming more aware of my thoughts and becoming more present each day. This stuff really works and I am in no way near to full experience yet, so excited for what is. I am at your 2nd Life Design Getaway day on June 21st 2013 so I anticipate an amazing experience there, too. Thank you very much, Andy.

3) *Hi Andy, I have been like a crab with the BUG FREE MIND process. Checking it all out from every angle. Firstly, downloading the free chapters in October 2012 and taking until end of January 2013 to read, understand, absorb and apply the teachings of each chapter. I then decided to purchase the course (books and audio) at the end of Jan 2013. From the moment of receiving the books and downloading the audio, my life is not the same as it used to be.*

I know I have finally found the link to massive quantum personal awareness and development. This man teaches differently, you will get this stuff, it will sink in and your life will be more focused, happy and driven in the most natural way. If you're here reading this, it's because you're meant to, so do yourself a favour and buy the system. Well worth it!

4) Hi Andy, I've been using the BUG FREE WORLD members' site now for almost a month. I have the books and the audio, too. Since I started to read and listen to your book(s), I have noticed a real shift in my day-to-day self-awareness and felt content with my progress.

However, when I joined the BUG FREE WORLD site, my understanding and absorption of the material has gone to another level. Almost like when I was back at school learning my favourite subject. Absolutely loving the journey. Thanks.

5) Hey Phil/Andy, Trust all is well and happy on planet bug free. I was so excited and happy to read about your fab manifestations on the site, regarding your big re-launch of ABFM. Your teachings are just what the world needs now. I am happy to be a part of that, thank-you.

So to the point of my contacting you... I have purchased the books, audios and the SMS video series. I am loving them all. I was also at your 2nd design getaway day in June. An immense day, which was inspiring and motivational for me. Thank-you.

On that day, I came away with a skeleton of a design for a city centre hair salon (Manchester). Since then, I have been working on my mind map for this and I have now finished it and I am ready to start manifesting on it. Indeed, there is an opportunity arising to purchase an on-going concern in the city centre. I have also been receiving emails from all agents in the area relating to either existing salons or empty units. I also have a great working relationship with my supplier who, in any event, will fit or re-fit any concern I enter into for free. So that's a great bit of manifesting already and I am still only on book one!!!

I have over 35 years experience in this industry and love each day I go to work, as it does not, and never has, felt like work. Love what you do, hey? I have a successful and profitable salon already in the Chorlton district of South Manchester. It is a small bijou salon but still can turn over a gross profit of £250,000 - £300,000 per annum after 10 years trading. I have had 5 salons in my lifetime, all providing me well at the time but, after time, I found myself somewhere else. I now KNOW I was looking for me, thanks to your books. I feel like I have such a lot more to achieve, before I hang my scissors up, as it were.

So there it is. My mind map is attached, as is my 32 year old daughter Nicola, as she will be helping to operate this and any future ventures I may have. Thank-you for your considerations and I will await patiently any comments or observations you may have. Cheers, Best wishes, Seamus.

6) Hi, Phil. I trust you are well and happy. Just a thought really, having seen some of the members on site attending the Life Design Getaway days. I attended the one in June of last year in Sussex. I came away with my design to open a city centre salon and to build a business with my daughter. You may remember I passed my mind maps of the design over to you, for Andy to look at them, to tighten them up, as it were.

Anyway, over these past 9 months, I had looked at 2 different sites but they didn't "feel" correct. Then a site I had always thought would make a great hairdresser's became available. A client of mine made me aware of it, out of the blue.

To cut a long story short, I am now 6 weeks away from opening the salon. It ticks off almost everything on my designs and, in the few areas it doesn't, I have realised that what I am creating here is the absolute solid foundation to certainly get me there. Having checked the demographics of the area, I found that 5,000 people walk past the unit each day. So it became a no brainer. To attract 0.01% of that footfall into my salon will make the concern immediately successful. That's without all of my other marketing advertising and research coming into play. My intuition moved me to act.

So to my point. The Life Design Getaway has worked for me and I have manifested it within a year. I am very happy about this and am very grateful to all you guys at ABFM.

I wondered if Andy might like to use my design as an example to Life Design Getaway attendees in the future, to show that what he is teaching actually works for real?

As I said, just a thought........ Cheers, Phil.

7) Hey, Andy. This all started for me last June 2013 in sunny Sussex at the Life Design Getaway I attended. This whole process of manifesting my design has been stress-free and without any resistance. It's almost like the place has fallen into my lap and, at each stage, stuff has just happened, or things have just turned up.

Yesterday for instance, my supplier gave me four free chair protector covers which I had desired, along with 10 free beautiful Italian hairdryer holders that I'd had my eye on and the best was a brand new £600 floor standing electric hair colour processor. All for free!!

It's like all sorts of stuff happening to help me achieve this with the least amount of effort. The solicitor acting for me reduced her bill by over £1,000 because I had the cheek to ask her. My marketing strategy has been a dream with campaigns ready to go at the touch of a button. I have secured high visibility positions on the students' union website, Manchester UNI intranet and Manchester Royal Infirmary intranet, too.

As in my design, people are just presenting themselves to me, "wanting" to work for me. Amazing, really. The list goes on and on. I am very happy. Thank you, Andy.

END

Do you see how Seamus was happy first, he was grateful, he designed what he wanted, then just went about creating it and making it as perfect as he could.

It wasn't impossible to find the city centre location but to have it show up at the right time was improbable. But because he thought it could, it did. When we get out of our own way, it allows our subconscious mind to do what it was designed to do.

Next, I'd like to share with you what Philip Wyatt shared on his blog in the community site. I asked Phil if he would mind if I shared it with you, as I think it is somewhat inspiring.

My positive changes so far

I have been on the Bug Free World now for nearly 3 years, one of the first, maybe. For any of you doubters out there, I would just like to run through some of the changes it has had in my world, some of the positive changes in my life and how everything has improved. I write this to not only help me in my never ending progress but to inspire you all to never ever give up:

Relationships

My partner loves me even more.

My children come to visit me more than they ever did and communicate by phone so much more.

My friends love me to organise get-togethers and motorcycle tours with them.

My communication skills have improved 10 fold due to my confidence improving every day. I am no longer scared to approach people and start a chat. I just listen so much better and am genuinely interested in other people's lives. I am able to help people and always go to give, I am liked for this. I never knowingly hurt another person, as I am aware that we are all connected and would therefore only be hurting myself.

I have forgiven everyone for any past hurts, including my parents. I no longer have any resentment towards another in any way and have no feelings of bitterness or revenge. Anyone who tries to hurt me in any way do not succeed, because I am aware that they are unconscious at the time and don't really know what they are doing, so therefore are easily forgiven.

I have learnt how to be completely calm in all situations, be transparent to any personal verbal attacks and criticisms just wash off me like water off a duck's back. I listen and concentrate on people's words and get to know them a lot better and even remember their names as a result.

Materialistic Improvements

I now live in a detached 4 bed house with two en-suites, double garage, dressing room and own office, (my dream house). I Drive a BMW X5 people carrier and have just ordered a brand new Ford Transit.

My business is going great and I have over 200 more clients than 2 years ago. My personal drawings have risen by over 30%. I have a brand new £13,000 motorbike and I am well on the way to finishing my mortgage payments.

I now have three holidays a year, already been to Southern Ireland and have booked up for Switzerland in July and Southern France in September. I am in the process of organising a Caribbean cruise for next year, on the biggest boat in the world. New Zealand is also on the agenda.

Self Improvement

Mastered No Mind for over 5 minutes and able to hold 15 minutes of positive thought.

I have absolutely no regrets from the past, have forgiven everybody and so I hold no resentment whatsoever.

I never criticise anymore and hardly ever judge a person but do a lot of observation. I never put another person down for trying and constantly praise other people's efforts. My thoughts towards others are always good and positive and I always go to give when meeting new people, as I know it always comes back to me in other ways (it certainly does).

I now have complete peace and easiness in my life, as I have learnt to accept my non peace. My constant feeling of dread and knotted stomach feeling has completely disappeared. I only think of calmness and therefore I am. I am always happy now, so therefore know that I will be happy in the future.

All my old feelings of fear, stress, anxiety, anxiousness and constant worry (all nasty feelings) have dissolved. They are just not there anymore. They were all mostly just habits and I became aware of this when I just looked at them. All that is left is peace, harmony, easiness and simplicity in my life. What do I have to worry about right now? Nothing. Ah, stress, you are after my attention! I know what all these negative feelings are trying to convey and so can easily beat them in an instant when they TRY to raise their ugly head.

I now accept everything from my past and any situation that arises. I just accept whatever the outcome is. I never resist or fight, to make the situation change. I look at it, knowing that whatever happens will be for the best and the best outcome. I know that whatever happens to me will be for the best, so I win every time, even if it looks like I have lost at the time. This is my form of surrender, not giving in but not resisting either!

Negativity is now a thing of the past. My thoughts are all positive and, if they are not, I am aware, due to me being predominately present and immediately swap the bad thought for a good one. My thought patterns have made me an optimist now and automatically positive most of the time. I wake up knowing my day is going to be great, thinking it is, feeling it is and guess what happens?

I no longer compete with others or in business, as I know it will always work out for the best and have no competitors, only myself. I never feel sorry for others, only compassion, I give out good thoughts to them, instead. I no longer use the words, or have the state of mind of hoping, wanting, needing or waiting. I only ever desire. I practise the art of gratitude and I appreciate all that I have but, at the same time, allow more goodness to appear in my life. If I ever desire anything, I visualise and imagine that I already have it. I am grateful, because it is already mine and show appreciation, because all I desire is reality to kick in.

I am totally aware of my ego and all its sneaky little tricks and never feel the need to argue. I know that repetition is a must for changing my thought patterns. Therefore, I concentrate on my thinking (being in the now) until it becomes an automatic default way of thinking. Cool and it works. I have questioned all my core beliefs and never use the word 'believe' as it is code for doubt and doubt is another word for fear (false evidence appearing real).

I am still working hard on removing my desire to please other people and be concerned about what other people think of me (this has been a hard nut for me to crack, but I am getting there), although I am nowhere near as embarrassed and self-conscious when talking in front of large groups anymore. I never ever blame anyone or myself and never play the blame game. It's pointless. I can now define what faith means to me and I have changed my belief I had to luck and now realise that so called luck is when opportunity meets chance. You make your own luck.

I now understand risk and realise that doing nothing (fear of loss) is far riskier than getting out there and acting on your desires. I have taken complete responsibility on all levels of my life. This has given me an inner type of power and invincibility. I understand the illusion of time and am now never busy and always have plenty of time for everything I have to accomplish. I never rush, never work hard and amazingly now never need to. I have made my life simple and uncluttered. Any jobs or tasks that must be done are imagined as if done already, gratefulness springs to mind, visualisation of the job complete becomes a default way of thinking and way hey, the task is complete, easily.

I have explored my own death and no longer fear it. I am happy now and therefore will be in the future, I choose to be calm now. I always look for the benefit and value in what I am doing and in all situations. I do not try to do anything; I either do it or I don't. I am aware that I don't know anything unless I apply it or am applying it, this is a great eye-opener for me.

I have learnt the art of manifesting (creating) by design and know that whatever you can conceive and know, you can create. I practise my designs on a regular basis. I know the benefits, the value. I make the steps for achievement and am grateful for them, both before and when they come into reality. I accept, allow and detach myself from the outcome, knowing for certain that the outcome will be the right one, or even better.

Conclusion

I know the above may seem like a lot of hard work for some but remember, there is no rush when you know you are on the right path. After searching for the answers for many years I knew this early on and therefore knew I could take it steady mastering each new skill as I went along. I was worth it and so are you.

My life is brilliant in every way, thanks to this system. Don't allow your ego to sabotage your efforts, keep at it for ever, there is nothing better out there. You will be that person you desire to be if you just get it all ingrained into your mind to such a level that you can write out what I just did without thinking too much. It is there in my head, I am living proof that it works. You too can have the life you desire, if only you carry on doing the easy steps involved.

Sorry this is a little long but you were meant to read this, I trust it has inspired you to keep at it. Good fortune to you all. Phil

END

Phil sharing that inspired me that my work is on track and delivering results. He has created for himself a way of life, which means that anything he desires, he can now manifest. He has created the environment, which means it all just works for him.

I'm sure you noticed as you read it that Phil was applying all what I'm teaching you here to make the law of attraction work for you.

I've included these two wonderful examples to demonstrate to you that you can desire to become the master of the law of attraction that I know you can be. That your work on yourself is essential for you achieving it.

You can learn how to use the tool fairly quickly. But where the real work is needed is on the environment in your mind and life. You fix that and it is impossible for you to not become a master, because this is a law and it has rules... It will work for you because it is neutral, l as we are going to cover right now...

Chapter 10:

The Law of Attraction is Neutral

In the last few chapters we've seen some amazing stories of great uses of the law of attraction. All of them have unfolded in a way that demonstrates a very similar pattern. Well, next I want to show you how neutral the law of attraction is and that you can use it just as easily to create bad stuff as you create good stuff... In exactly the same way as the Russian guy on the train did...

You've seen me do some things which make me look pretty good, right? Well, this is going to make me look like a muppet creating some bad magic...

Here's a situation where I am using the law of attraction currently to solve the damage I did by using the law to create the problem in the first place.

My friend, Phil, has witnessed first hand the 'magic' I can create with my computers. He has seen this 'magic', as has my wife, my friend Martin and even the computer service company I use. All have said that the problems (magic) are not possible. Yet, at different times, they have all seen with their own eyes this 'magic' happening on my computers. Then, as they sat in my chair, as if by 'magic' again, the problem vanished. Now I'm not saying this has happened once or twice. I am talking about hundreds and hundreds of times that I have created magical impossibilities.

In fact, in 2010, one of my primary goals was to become competent here and stop creating these problems (this magic) and I have worked towards this goal. It has not been an instant thing for me but I have seen a point at which I do not create these 'magical' problems any more. Now, the occurrences of these 'truly remarkable' phenomena had already diminished substantially by mid 2010. After that, I was only able to work magic on odd occasions, which is of course good as this is very bad magic!

I tracked the problem back, to work out how I created it in the first place. The real problem was I became unconscious when I created each instance, or I turned a normal problem into one of these magical problems as well.

I am obviously a bit of a control freak and I recognised, thanks mainly to a friend who noticed that my frustration with computers was that I was out of control, and I had to ask for another person's help to solve it. This created two problems for me, I don't like to ask for help (a weakness) and I am annoyed at myself for not having studied more, so that I did not need help (stupid and judgemental).

So I was not accepting what is, and I was not fully surrendering to the problem. Over the first few months of 2010, the occurrences of the magical problems began falling away to probably less than one major incident a month (could have been three times a week, before!). And normal-sized computer frustration is now only maybe once weekly. What's more, when they occur, I am present on many more of the occasions, so I do not allow myself to get angry and frustrated. The magic then seems to vanish - not always, but more frequently - *I am still on the journey, remember!*

When I am not present and I do allow myself to get frustrated and angry then, afterwards, I see that I did it and observe my reactions to it. All in all, I would say I have killed off the horror I had with this and I am well on my way to realising fully the resolution of this 100%. In other words, I am well on the way to stopping creating more bad magic.

It's four years now since I killed off the majority of this bad magic problem. I probably have two or three times a year now that something unreal happens and I created a routine for myself of noticing it, relaxing, doing something else and expecting the problem to resolve itself.

Sure enough, this has worked and I was able to change my thinking, so that I stopped creating the problem. Because I was the controller of my world and if I actually knew that, then I could change things. So I did, I finally figured out how to use this tool to stop harming myself too! I used time, routines and my knowledge of brain plasticity to stop myself doing something really dumb and my enjoyment in life has grown, thanks to stopping this very bad magic.

So Where Are You Practising Bad Magic?

If you analyse your past, then you will find times where the law of attraction has been in use by you to create some pretty bad magic!

Just imagine the guy on the train for a second, observe what thoughts and feelings must have gone through his mind to create that much bad magic. This guy was an incredible practitioner where it comes to the law of attraction. But we all have the same skill. Let me show you a quick example where the mass audience is using it to negative effect: -

"I can't leave my job, I'm stuck here"

They are creating the feeling of being trapped, which is a very powerful and effective use of the law of attraction. They are very good at using the law to create the life they *don't* '*want.*' This is because people only know 'specifically' what they don't 'want' and do not really know 'specifically' what they desire. So then, they cannot create anything other than what they know. Therefore, they are using the law just to create some really bad stuff. They are practising 'bad magic!'

If you were to ask a cancer doctor who deals with patients with bad cancer, which of their patients are going to make it through, they would quickly say they didn't know! But if you probed further, then they would also say, *'The ones who were more positive-thinking or optimistic had a much better chance.'* I am also sure that if studies were, or have been done on this, then the statistics would show this to be very true. Consider for a second where medicine would be now if Émile Coués' work had been adopted worldwide by the medical profession…

So just by thinking differently, we can actually get worse or get better. Well hang on a minute, can we see an example of this in any of the times we have been ill in the past? *'I'm not going to let this cold beat me'* or *'I'm really sick!'* So you must act as if you already have what you want – because you already do have it. Stop practising 'bad magic!'

At the moment, I'm teaching my children to play pool. They keep saying, *"I can't do these sort of shots."* To which I say, *"No, you haven't been able to do those shots yet!"* This is basic stuff but we tell our subconscious minds what we want them to hear, IF we are conscious and aware of our thoughts. It is obvious we do not wish to program our minds to fail but it is with equal ease we can program them to succeed.

I have not banned the word 'can't' in our household but I do use the use of it as a way point to show when *thinking is crooked.* Why not consider noticing your use of the word 'can't' and see what instructions you are sending to your subconscious mind when you do… Then why not consider making some small language changes that, over time, will move the neurons around in your brain and deliver you the result you desire, rather than create more bad magic you don't want. *If you think you can't or you can, you're right!*

The law of attraction is totally neutral; you can use it to create all wonderful things in life, or you can use it to create and perpetuate pain. It is just a tool after all and you are the craftsman.

The question to next consider is the future you, thank-you for taking the time out to change the little things in life that pull you off-track, so that your whole life pulls in the right direction…

We're nearing the end now and next I want to give you the process you need to apply   to   become   the   master   you   were   designed   to   be.

Chapter 11:

Mastering the Law of Attraction

I'm going to keep this simple, as it is simple. Because we do not shut off our mind's *doubts*, they have so many hours a day to complicate everything. So what I want to do here is bring all the lessons together and make it so that you can keep practising this to become the master.

If you find you are still struggling, then you'll be doing one or more of the elements below wrongly and so will need to go back and re-read to change that part. But if you start small then you'll find that this technique will work and you'll get better and then much better at it. So much so, that you'll notice you created some pretty big stuff, after it's happened.

So we'll run through it first, then I'll give you a few small things to go and create to practise building and honing the new mental pathways you've nurtured into existence.

Do you remember this?

To create what you desire with your thoughts, you have to have attained a state of mind where you have actually had it happen and felt it happen in your mind. And, in that process, you become detached from it because you have already had it. Then what happens is you work diligently on making that a reality for everyone else, as it is already a reality in your mind. And you keep going until you get there! This is how we create.

Ok, let's create a process for it. But don't try too hard with this, as it's a guideline, which you will use to guide your feelings into the creation of what you desire.

Here's a 5-step process to create anything you truly desire

<u>Step 1.</u> You first have to think up what you want, a new car, a holiday, meet someone, solve a problem, a little extra money, a new job, an extra job, an invitation to something, or something bigger like a new business, your perfect partner, an idea that will change the world.

You first have to find something that you truly desire and, if it's something big, then it has to be something you are prepared to attempt even if you die whilst spending your life in its attainment!

But if it's something smaller, then you still have to keep going UNTIL you get it, as time is not important. The desire to have it accomplished is the important bit.

Remember the kudos I sought in the attainment of becoming a millionaire. Or the refusal to live my life without a cure.

You want to have a keen pulsating desire for something big. Not something you would like. This is essential for your success in becoming the master. On the smaller stuff, you don't need this desire in the same way... because the smaller stuff is much easier to conceive as possible and even probable.

Step 2. You have to travel forward in time with your mind and experience the feeling of having had whatever you desire to have happened already. So that you feel that it happened a few minutes ago, a few months ago, or a few years ago. But that it <u>has happened</u>.

You want to experience how it feels now that it's happened, see how happy you are with yourself for manifesting it. Be there. Experience it.

Feel how grateful you are that it's now in your life and how grateful you are that you demonstrated to yourself that you could change your world with just your mind.

See how long it took to happen and how it didn't happen until it was the perfect time and in the perfect way. Feel how relaxed you feel knowing now that time wasn't important.

Look at how it came into your life, you're just dreaming so it could've come in any way, as it's just one of the possible ways and doesn't have to be the way... Feel how it all sort of fell into place. Feel how right it feels that you designed having it, and then got it, and how it just now feels part of your life experience.

Fill your mind with details about how it all feels for you having had it. Remind yourself how it felt the day you got it. What a sense of accomplishment that was. How great that made you feel. How you were able to use your success to inspire you to greater success...

You keep staying here thinking about it, UNTIL you feel that you've had it.

I will say that again just in case you missed it, as it's **essential** for your success...

You keep staying here thinking about it, UNTIL you feel that you've had it.

When you've felt that you've had it, then you can move to step 3, not before.

This can take as little as 10 minutes, or a period of time longer than that. Basically, it doesn't matter how long it takes, *as you can't skip this!* So you have to have it have happened in your mind first. I trust I have made my point.

Step 3. This bit won't make sense and won't work unless you've had step 2 happen… Now consider, after you've had it happen for real in your mind… do you actually really need this to happen in reality?

Think about it for a while, it's just become real to you, so it's real. Do you still need it? Sure you'd like it but you don't need it. Can you feel why not?

The feeling you should be experiencing is one of, *'well this is obviously going to happen at the right time and in the right way. It will happen when it's best for it to happen for me.'*

Can you feel it? That's the feeling you are looking to have in your mind. Do not move on until you get it. To get it just keep running step 2 and 3 until you have it happen. Or if you're okay with not mastering the law of attraction, then move on. A choice and, as usual, choice is the problem and the solution.

When you have that feeling, you have created the magical part of the law of attraction *as you are both attached to your dream or desire and detached from it at exactly the same time.* This is demonstrating abundance to the universe and showing your subconscious mind what to get you in a very cool and relaxed way. For anything you've attained in life, you achieved this feeling and mind state before you got it.

Step 4. You begin taking the appropriate actions you can take to bring it into everyone else's reality. For me, the appropriate action with A Bug Free Mind, was to write the process, the book. For me, the appropriate action to find the perfect partner was to look at the people I passed by. For me the appropriate action with becoming rich was to evaluate all my options for making money and then settle on investing in Real Estate.

With each thing I set out to achieve, I filled my mind with research on that subject and became an expert in it in a very short period of time. I made what I desired my dominant thought and focused. But I did it without needing, without wanting in a very relaxed, detached but focused way. That's how you go about creating what you desire.

I was just working diligently on what I desired, keeping my eyes wide open and expecting manufactured coincidences to 'just happen'. Because I was expecting my dream and desire to give me plenty of things to help it come into everyone else's reality, I was then of course rewarded by seeing coincidences begin happening everywhere. When I notice a coincidence, I see it as probably me manifesting it… I do not need to know it is. I choose to look at it that way, as it helps. Do I have any proof? No! Do I need any? Definitely not; only my ego would need proof.

I gratefully accept the coincidence and consider that this was me manifesting it. I think the coincidence will help, so of course it does. My confidence is automatically growing with each little step of the manifestation.

Step 5. You keep going, until the reality in your mind has been brought into everyone else's reality too. So you simply choose to keep going, UNTIL... At this point you use this consideration to keep your mind focused... *"If it hasn't happened yet, then it's either not supposed to, or I've missed something. Let's go and see if I've missed something." "After all, it's going to happen at the best time and in the best way for me, so I wonder what I've yet to learn."*

I've used that countless times when I've wobbled on my resolve.

The funny thing is, you are not looking to force your manifestation into existence. You are looking to apply less effort and more consideration to the subject. As you do, then you'll find it'll sometimes make things pop up from fresh air.

Remember to take breaks from it when you feel like it. You don't think I wrote this book in one sitting do you? No, it took me a few days and, when I felt tired or wrong in any way, I simply stopped and allowed myself time to return to my full potential.

Observe how you feel and watch out for your ego attempting to throw doubts at you. Do not force these doubts out of your mind. Just see them for what they are, *'useless and destructive at getting you what you desire.'*

So you simply carry on working diligently on manufacturing coincidences and bringing what you've had in your mind into our reality. It's not a question of giving up. The only reason to stop is when you genuinely have no desire for it to happen any more. Then the funny thing with that is, sometimes it'll still happen anyway, after you've given up.

But if you give up knowing this doesn't work, then you'll be right. A choice!

Lastly...

The manifestation process can always produce you something bigger and better, too... So always be open for a greater manifestation.

People often ask me, so how do I make sure I never give up on my dream? The answer is *you cannot give up on something that has become real to you.* So make it real to you and then get on with it.

Some things to practise building your mental muscles with...

As with all things big and small, remember this; that you must know that if you can think it up, it's already created as a possibility. It may not be a probability but that's okay. Your job is to just stack the odds as much as you reasonably can to shorten the odds on the probability.

So I suggest you start small, as these things will convince you of your power to manifest. Then when you attain more confidence in your ability, then you dare to dream bigger... And you'll have more ammunition with which to fight your ego.

Manifest this - Decide to create an extra £150 or $200 in your life through something happening.

Manifest this - Decide to have a chance meeting with someone who will inspire you and so their presence will convince you that you can manifest. They don't need to be famous, just that they say or do something that you notice as something you asked for.

Manifest this - Decide to have a more pleasurable journey than you used to expect when you next travel to work, or anywhere. Then decide to always have pleasurable journeys...

Manifest this - Decide to have more good things just happen to you, see yourself as being happier because of all the good things that have happened.

Manifest this - Decide that someone you know is going to call you... Or contact you in some way.

Run the full 5-step manifestation process for each of those, or one of them at a time. Your choice... You won't get this wrong, just have fun and play as the child you once were.

Give yourself a break and remember to always be delighted with yourself. Time does not matter, your success does and success is *inevitable* and a process you will attain, if you just continue to do *the right things in the right way.*

Bigger dreams

When it comes to dreaming bigger, create your dreams so that you get them automatically but that you go to give. For example, if you are in business and you wish to increase your customers, think about how your goods or service will benefit those people. See their lives having benefitted from your help. How does that make you feel? You feel good, right? Then focus on seeing the benefits in your service for others and you'll create more people to serve.

Consider this. Do you think I sat there and saw the benefit I'd be bringing to your life, before you came to find my work... Sure I did, I filled my mind with seeing the benefits I bring to people's lives. It inspires me to continue working on my dream.

Do you think that by helping enough people, I will get the financial rewards I seek? Sure it does, but as Wallace Wattles said in the Science of Getting Rich, *"Give every man more in use value than you take from him in cash value; then you are adding to the life of the world by every business transaction"* I don't just think and know that, I live it as *a way of life.*

Take the price of this book as an example. Work out what it cost you in cash paid to me, and the cost of the time you spend reading it . Let's call it $150. Well, if you only apply the first item in the list of small things to manifest, you'll have more than that back. Look to give more and attempt to outgive the universe if you can... though I've not yet found it can be done, as you always receive more than you give out.

So if you focus on going to give, and not going to get, then you will get automatically. This is living to the virtue of selfishness where, with every transaction, you add more value than you are taking in remuneration.

This is living to abundance, always see abundance and abundance will slowly begin to appear at the right time and in the right way. Then, when it does choose to show up, you'll have more than you'll ever need. As long as you think you will, that is!

Chapter 12:

A Few Helpful Things for You to Consider While You Are Becoming a Law of Attraction Master

I've summarised a lot of the work I've created for you here and you can use it to keep your mind in tune. Bob Proctor said, *"Repetition is the first law of learning"*, and if you want to be able to live your life to the *way of life* I've described to you here, then you may wish to consider these points a few times each week to help you on your journey to *Mastering The Law of Attraction...*

Consider, I can change my world if I think I can and if I do not doubt it. I must choose to remember this and observe my ego, to see if I am actually living to this as *a way of life*.

Consider, am I living to the truth of the law in step 1 of the 5 step process in chapter 11, or am I just attempting to know it?

Consider, my thoughts govern my life... am I living to this...

Consider, I am a creator; I create in my life situations and circumstances which are in harmony with my dominant thoughts. How does this make you feel...

Consider your state of thought; know that you create, so consider what you are creating...

Consider, if you can conceive your future, then it exists as a potential reality and all you have to do now is bring it into reality. You just need to know it's real, that you can create your chosen outcome and exactly how you must set about doing it on purpose.

Consider, make sure you are in the right place to create from, ask yourself often, *"Am I at ease with this moment?"* And ask yourself often, *"What is going on inside me at the moment?"*

Consider, if it's not working, is it just not working yet - check your environment is right in your mind...

Consider, am I choosing to be happy now...

Consider, am I remembering to practise being grateful...

Consider, am I worrying about time...

Consider, if it hasn't happened yet, then what do I still have to learn… Remember to accept it as it is and remain delighted with yourself, no matter what…

Consider, are you still living to the fact that everything will always work out for the best for you… That everything will happen at exactly the right time and in exactly the right way for you… How does this make you feel…

As you change your perception of the law of attraction, from one of thinking that something on the outside is what matters, to understanding that it all comes from the inside of you, it frees you up to understand that you have the power over it all. If, that is, you decide you do.

Here's some real words of wisdom to inspire you, from someone who had one of the greatest mindsets I've ever seen…

"Impossible is just a big word thrown around by small men who find it easier to live in the world they've been given than to explore the power they have to change it. Impossible is not a fact. It's an opinion. Impossible is not a declaration. It's a dare. Impossible is potential. Impossible is temporary. Impossible is nothing." Muhammad Ali

The impossible is possible for you, if you think it is. If you do not, then you should give up and just enjoy being where you are instead, as you'll avoid a lot of frustration!

But if you do think the impossible is possible, then be grateful for all you have and all that is coming to you. But do not need it. Just be grateful for what you have already had happen in your mind. You are showing your subconscious what you desire, by having it already.

Nearly all the time I'm working on it, I am grateful for what's coming in my Bug Free Mind journey and I'm grateful for it in a lot of the time I'm not working on it. I work and live in *a state of gratefulness*; it's simply *my way of life*.

I am not in a rush to get there, as it's happening fast enough. If anything, I'd like to slow it down, so I can savour it more. I want to enjoy all of my life on my journey and A Bug Free Mind is only part of my life, not all of it.

Your main desires will be part of your life, not all of it… A Bug Free Mind will be the thing I'm remembered for but my family and friends and experiences are what we do the things we want to do for, anyway.

When I made my first fortune, I was in such of a rush to get to the next part of the journey that I didn't enjoy where I was each time I did something big. My friend Phil said to me once, *"I got the best out of you having all those supercars. I got the pleasure, the experience. You were too busy being busy to enjoy them."* He was right and I'll say as the Jews said, Never Again!

This life is the one life you are living now, so live it now. Enjoy the moments and you'll be given more moments to enjoy. Master the law of attraction, create an amazing life for yourself but live in the moments, as they are gone in no time.

If you have enjoyed learning this and you would like to see just how powerful you really are, and what level you can take your life to, then I strongly suggest you begin the Bug Free Mind Process; it was my ulterior motive for sharing all this work with you. Because if you think what I've taught you here is clever, then trust me, you ain't seen nothing yet!

You can get the first 5 chapters free from www.ABugFreeMind.com and you will see instant results and will want more, as I think you'll agree it is the missing piece of the puzzle.

I look forward to speaking with you again soon; your friend and guide, Andy.

More on the law of attraction in A Bug Free Mind

In the Bug Free Mind Process, I cover a lot of what I've covered here on mastering the law of attraction. I also cover the whole of life, finding your purpose and, as Buddha put so well, I show how to create an end to suffering. Anyone who's read it will tell you, if anything, I'm playing down the benefits of reading, listening or watching the Process.

The Process comes in books and audios for the fastest way to get it into your life as *a way of life*. I suggest reading and listening to it, as I teach all the aspects of Structured Thinking for every area of life to ensure the very best life possible.

Click here to learn more

Then, as *a way of life,* there is nothing better than my Success Made Simple video course, where the purpose of the course is to really change the wiring of your mind by focusing on two or three really small bits of wisdom each week. These take 3 to 8 minutes each to watch and a few minutes longer to think about.

The purpose is not to get to the end of this course; the purpose is to create *a successful way of life.* And during the trial, you'll see how beneficial this is.

Click here to learn more

Then the only other thing I offer is the recordings of a one-day course on designing anything you want. I demonstrate what cannot be covered effectively in words how to design anything.

Included in that is the design for my perfect partner, Alison, how to design the impossible and make it happen and a lot more.

Click here to learn more

The Bug Free Mind Process in any form is available to you all the time. So it's ready for when you want to begin.

Whatever you do I strongly suggest you download and read the 5 free chapters, as this will tell you if you are ready to begin now or later. Click here for the 5 Free Chapters

But just so I am being completely straight with you, *all wish they had begun sooner!* Virtually everyone goes through the process multiple times, as this is not just a book or audio to read and consume like all the others.

This is about creating a way of life, which results in your ultimate success. As I say in the process, the only time you'll have finished with this is when you have created the success you desire.

So if you're ready for your ultimate success, then you can get started on the process today by going to www.ABugFreeMind.com

Made in the USA
Las Vegas, NV
10 March 2021

19352872R00056